BER

Please renew/return items by last date
shown. Please call the number below:

Renewals and enquiries: 0300 1234049

Textphone for hearing or
speech impaired users: 01992 555506

www.hertfordshire.gov.uk/libraries
L32

532 565 45 7

What a wonderful world

What a wonderful world

Good news stories to calm your mind for a peaceful night's sleep

HarperCollins*Publishers*

HarperCollins*Publishers*
1 London Bridge Street
London SE1 9GF

www.harpercollins.co.uk

HarperCollins*Publishers*
1st Floor, Watermarque Building, Ringsend Road
Dublin 4, Ireland

First published by HarperCollins*Publishers* 2022

1 3 5 7 9 10 8 6 4 2

© HarperCollins Publishers 2022

Illustrations: Shutterstock.com

Nikki Girvan asserts the moral right to
be identified as the author of this work

A catalogue record of this book is
available from the British Library

ISBN 978-0-00-849835-1

Printed and bound in the UK using 100%
renewable electricity at CPI Group (UK) Ltd

MIX
Paper from
responsible sources
FSC™ C007454

This book is produced from independently certified FSC™ paper
to ensure responsible forest management.

For more information visit: www.harpercollins.co.uk/green

For all the activists, artists, scientists and everyday folk who make the world a better place – and those who tell their stories. This book wouldn't exist without you. Keep spreading joy, hope and inspiration and shining a light in the dark.

Contents

Introduction

In this modern world, it can feel like a good night's sleep is hard to come by. Even when we retreat to the private and intimate sanctuary of our bedrooms, we take with us blue-lit windows onto tragedy, devastation and destruction that unfold every single day, all around the world.

Hardwired to recognise threats to our existence, doomscrolling late into the night has become a dangerous collective pastime, one that plays havoc with our circadian rhythms – the 24-hour cycles that are part of our body's internal clock and essential to our health and wellbeing – raising levels of stress hormones such as cortisol and rendering a good night's sleep nigh on impossible.

And it's not just bad news that keeps us up at night. The ease with which our thumbs habitually guide us from news apps to social media feeds, work emails to text messages and – arguably the most disruptive creation of all – family WhatsApp groups, at the very time we most want to relax is disconcerting to say the least. Thankfully, with practice, habits can be broken and the solution is already in your hands.

The benefits of reading *any* book before bedtime have long been extolled by experts – according to research from the University of Sussex just six minutes of reading can reduce stress levels by 68 per cent. This book gently encourages you to spend those daily few minutes (or more) focusing on the positive goings-on in the world, because they do exist. This is a helpful, hopeful reminder that only when we look up from the distress displayed on our devices will we notice the positive steps being taken together too.

From environmental advances such as military bases being transformed into wildlife sanctuaries and smart tech firms saving the world's honeybees, to extraordinary people volunteering their time to set up charities and helplines to lend a helping hand, there are acts of kindness and constant improvements being made in this world all the time. We just need to set aside a few minutes to acknowledge them.

This book is a salve for anxious minds. They might not have made the headlines, but every story within these pages is true. The hope is that you will find comfort in your new nightly habit and instead of the heaviness experienced after a dose of doom, you will start to feel a little lighter before turning out the light.

So disconnect, dip in and drift away into these bite-sized tales of hope and wake up refreshed to take on the world anew.

Military Bases Transformed into Wildlife Sanctuaries

Once no-go military zones at the height of the Cold War, sites along the border of the former Iron Curtain in Germany have been given a new lease of life. Some 62 former military bases, which once served as defences between East and West Germany during four decades of conflict, are now home to eagles, woodpeckers, bats, beetles and more, after the government decided to convert the unused sites into nature reserves, with some parts also open for public use.

Collectively, the sites cover 31,000 hectares (120 square miles) – the equivalent of 310,000 Olympic-sized swimming pools – and contain a diverse array of meadows, forests and marshes – the perfect environment for rare flora and fauna to thrive. The transformation has increased the total area dedicated to protected wildlife in Germany by a quarter. More than 30 years on from the reunification of the country, the land running along what was once referred to as 'the death strip' – owing to the many lives lost by those trying to cross the border – is now teeming with life and hope.

Smart Tech is Saving the Bees

Far from just being humble producers of honey, bees are responsible for a third of the food we eat, spreading pollen from flower to flower and triggering the growth mechanism that creates fruits, vegetables, nuts and seeds. Although the threats of pests, parasites and climate change have had a detrimental effect on the population of honeybees, they are now finding an unexpected saviour in smart tech.

An Irish company called ApisProtect (*apis* meaning bee in Latin) has developed sensors that can be placed under the roof of a beehive to monitor factors including temperature, humidity, sound and movement. Data from more than 400 smart sensor units, installed in hives managed by 20 commercial beekeepers across the US, Ireland, the UK and South Africa, is now transferred via the cloud to ApisProtect's headquarters in Cork. After being processed and analysed, actionable insights are sent back to the beekeepers, giving them a better understanding of bee health and productivity, allowing them to prevent problems such as changes in temperature or humidity, before they take hold.

Although a leader in their field, monitoring over 20 million honeybees, ApisProtect is not alone in using smart tech to help create larger, healthier colonies of bees. The Austrian HIVEOPOLIS research project (beehives of the future) has developed a dance robot bee, which is able to direct forager bees towards nectar or pollen sources and away from areas affected by dangerous pesticides, while Bulgarian Pollenity's Beebot is a personal intercom for hobbyist beekeepers' smart hives, which records changes in temperature and humidity and performs acoustic analysis every 15 minutes.

Smart tech is now officially the bee's knees.

LED Lights Lead the Way
for Bats

A Dutch town has introduced red streetlights as part of a sustainable housing development to meet the needs of some very special winged residents.

The town of Nieuwkoop in South Holland is the first in the world to introduce bat-friendly red LED streetlights after planning for a sustainable housing development revealed that the proposed site was next door to a nature reserve and important feeding ground for a number of rare species of bat.

As part of a network of nature protection areas across Europe, where many rare and threatened species of wildlife can be found, the town was no stranger to addressing conservation concerns. Realising that typical white streetlights would affect both the bats' nocturnal behaviour and where they would fly in the ecosystem (as they would be attracted by their insect prey congregating around the lights), the developers turned to the experts for advice.

Working with light technology specialists Signify, Wageningen University (WUR) and non-governmental organisations (NGOs) working on conservation projects, they have developed a solution using red LED lights that use a wavelength that doesn't interfere with the bats' internal compass. The LEDs also provide light that is useful for the area's human residents, and to which their eyes can easily adapt, acting like an automatic white balance in a camera, altering perception so that they will no longer notice the red colour.

As well as making the area hospitable for the bat community and ensuring the roads and pavements are safe, the innovative light installation also reduces the area's carbon footprint and energy consumption. The smart LED technology enables local authorities to remotely monitor and manage the lighting system, shutting it off completely late at night or turning lights on fully in the event of an emergency. They can even respond to resident requests to turn up or lower the brightness, so that the lights are only used when needed.

Japan's Senior Cheer Squad Smashes Stereotypes in Sequins

Japan is one of the world's most rapidly ageing nations, but one group steadfastly refuses to be limited or defined by their age – Japan Pom Pom. With members ranging from ages 60 to 89, cheer squad Japan Pom Pom is smashing stereotypes in sequins, mini-skirts and glitter as they perform on TV programmes and in popular charity shows.

The troupe's 89-year-old founder Fumie Takino came up with the idea more than 25 years ago, after seeing a cheer squad made up of senior citizens on the international news, but wasn't happy when the media dubbed her group the 'granny cheer dancers'.

Although now a grandma and great-grandma, Fumie is a great deal more than that and inspires other members to 'try anything' – just as she has. Her adventures include gaining her master's degree in America in her 50s, scuba diving, parasailing, playing the ukulele, skydiving, studying Spanish, dance classes and walking, ending each day with a small glass of beer.

The troupe is well-known for their 'unbelievably showy' performance outfits, which include sequinned cheer costumes, leather biker jackets, shades and silver wigs. Although frequently featured in positive government leaflets about active senior citizens, some more conservative groups maintain stereotypical views on life in old age and criticise the squad's outfits and performances. Despite this, the cheer squad's numbers have grown from five to 17 – all of whom had to audition for their place – with many stating that practising as a group gives them a boost and a purpose. They also extol the benefits of Fumie's positive outlook and are willing her to cheer on until she's 100.

Flower Power Brings Hope

As villages across Kerala, South India, shut down during the COVID-19 lockdown, the women of Chennam Pallippuram found a way to bring hope, colour and a source of income to their home – by transforming their village into a beautiful flowerbed.

Marigolds, oleanders and jasmine were planted in every corner of the *panchayat* or village council's 17 wards, providing employment for 340 women, who worked to cultivate 34 hectares (85 acres) of land. The women were paid for their time and the flowers were sold for use in temple rituals and functions such as weddings, with residents enjoying a good return due to demand.

The flower farming initiative was part of a state government project launched to fight food scarcity and convert uncultivated land into farms. Its success and popularity with the women of Chennam Pallippuram has led to a second phase of the project being planned, with large-scale vegetable farming set to be added so more women will benefit from the scheme.

From small seeds grow great ideas.

Mobile Bike Shop Brings Cycling to Navajo Nation

For many years, in the 70,9065 square kilometre (27,400 square mile) Native American territory of *Naabeehó Bináhásdzo* or the Navajo Nation, there wasn't a single bicycle shop. That was until a non-profit organisation called Silver Stallion Bicycle & Coffee Works rode into action.

Based in the city of Gallup, New Mexico, the team at Silver Stallion were aware of the inequity that was preventing children and adults in the Navajo Nation from taking up bike riding. However, only when bike shops and repair services were deemed essential during the pandemic, were they able to take significant action to address the problem.

After highlighting the lack of services to state authorities in the context of the global health emergency, the organisation received a $10,000 grant from the New Mexico Economic Development Department to allow them to establish a mobile bike repair centre to provide free bike repairs for people across the *Diné* (Navajo) land. On hearing of the project, more organisations pitched in to help, with the Southwest Indian Foundation donating a delivery truck that was later fitted out as a mobile workshop and the Catena Foundation providing the Silver Stallion team with an additional grant to cover the truck's operating costs.

The organisation then assembled a team of experts willing to donate their time, including mobile ride mechanic Manny Chavaria, who had recently opened the first bike shop in an area close to the Navajo Nation, designated for the Hopi and Arizona Tewa people. The team also salvaged parts from old bikes to manage the repairs and collected donated parts from other local businesses.

Using the initial grant, the organisation repaired 425 bikes over the course of 13 different events, in seven communities across the Navajo Nation. It looks to be just the start of a promising and vital initiative, with the scheme also encouraging others to act. Free Bikes 4 Kidz New Mexico has launched a donation drive aiming to collect 500 used bikes to be refurbished and provided to children in need, along with free helmets.

Speaking to Outside Online about the mobile bike shop project, Silver Stallion cofounder Scott Nydam said: 'If it's an essential service, it's a right to have. If there's a systemic reason for these things not existing in places like the Navajo Nation, there needs to be a systems approach towards addressing that.'

Period Pants Save Female-led Factory

A female-led garment factory in Shenzhen, southeastern China, found itself at risk of closure after the 2020 pandemic brought production almost to a halt. With existing orders cancelled and no sign of new ones, the excess fabric it housed was unlikely to be used and it seemed almost certain that the factory would close, jobs would be lost and the material would be sent to landfill.

In a last-ditch attempt, the factory's owner reached out to a neighbouring business, the manufacturing facility of a small UK-based sustainable period underwear company, WUKA, and asked if the company would buy the fabric.

Knowing that disposable period products take 500 years to decompose, the thought of the excess synthetic fabric – which could take between 20 and 200 years to decompose – not being used and polluting the planet did not sit right with them, so WUKA – which stands for Wake Up Kick Ass – decided to help.

The company created a unique design and repurposed the polyester to make 17,000 pairs of period pants, saving hundreds of jobs and ensuring that the material would not go to landfill. They donated 2,000 pairs of pants to Days for Girls International, a non-profit fighting for menstrual equity. They also launched a crowdfunding campaign in the UK, where people could donate £5 to cover the cost of providing an NHS worker with a free pair of period pants. The campaign raised more than £2,000 and allowed them to give 400 pairs to the NHS, while further pairs were also donated to Bloody Good Period, Women's Aid, Freedom for Girls and The Hygiene Bank.

The remaining period pants were made available on the company's website and also given away free with any orders placed on Earth Day 2021, to encourage customers to contribute to its survival, thereby saving the neighbouring factory and its employees from devastation. Speaking about the project, WUKA CEO Ruby Raut said: 'This all came about by following our principles, not knowing how the financial risk for us would work out. We managed to save the factory and ended up creating a style our customers loved. As a result, we are now in the process of creating a new supply chain for diverting fabrics destined for landfill, fast fashion marketplaces or to be incinerated so that we can save them to turn into planet-friendly period pants.'

Rhinos Are on the Up

A national rhino count in Nepal in 2021 found that the population of endangered one-horned rhinos in the country had increased by 16 per cent over six years. The count estimated that there were 752 rhinos, up 107 from a count in 2015 and a huge hike from numbers counted in the 1960s, when the population had dwindled to around 100.

The search was conducted by the country's Department of National Parks and Wildlife Conservation and undertaken by 350 people. Authorities and conservation groups attributed the growth in numbers to the protection of the animals and habitat management.

But the count wasn't the only good news for rhinos. In 2020, Kenya reported no cases of rhino poaching for the first time since 1999. Instances of poaching plummeted to zero from a high of 59 in 2013. This victory came through strengthening anti-poaching laws and increased patrols within wildlife habits. The Kenya Wildlife Service is now working to achieve the same zero-poaching goal for elephants in the country.

Wind Power Island Set to Blow Us Away

After building the world's first offshore wind farm in 1991, Denmark is aiming for yet another world-leading wind power project – by creating an island in the wind.

The $34 billion project – the largest construction project in Danish history – will see the first ever artificial island created to support a network of hundreds of wind turbines. Set in the North Sea, the 'energy island' will be built 50 miles west of Jutland, a low-lying peninsula in western Denmark. The first phase will be as big as 450 tennis courts and will act as a transmission centre for 200 wind turbines, each standing 260 metres (850 feet) tall, with the project expected to triple in size.

Described as a 'hub and spoke' energy scheme, the island will play the part of energy hub, with interconnectors to bordering North Sea countries. At first it will be capable of producing three gigawatts of electricity – enough to power up to 900,000 homes with renewable energy. However, there are plans to increase capacity over time to produce up to 10 gigawatts of energy, which is nearly one-and-a-half times Denmark's current needs. The island will also feature large batteries to store surplus electricity to meet spikes in demand.

The transformational project, which when fully implemented will be able to supply ten million European households, could be just the first in a network of hubs. The project also aims to use the artificial island to produce green hydrogen from seawater, to export for use across the globe.

Announced a year after Denmark's introduction of a cut-off date of 2050 for oil and gas extraction in the North Sea, Danish Minister of Climate and Energy and Public Utilities Dan Jørgensen described the project as 'a great moment for Denmark and for the global green transition'. The consortium behind the energy scheme, the North Sea Wind Power Hub programme, has also highlighted global ambitions for the project and the impact that it could have on fulfilling the European Union's aim to depend entirely on renewable energy by 2031.

Boys Club Boots Out Banter and Embraces Real Talk

Historically, the phrase 'boys club' might have conjured up images of laddish hijinks, pints being swigged and sports-based small talk. But a Dublin-based boys club is breaking free from these stereotypes in pursuit of better mental health for its members.

The Dublin Boys Club describes itself as a 'nomadic man's group exploring healthy masculinity' and has three important rules: no banter, no booze and keep it real and personal. The club is an offshoot of the Berlin Boys Club, established by Irish meditation teacher, Conor Creighton, while living in the German city. Concerned by rising suicide levels, anxiety and depression among men, he aimed to create a safe space for men – initially strangers – to come together, open up and practise real talk.

When Conor moved back to Ireland he brought the club home with him and opened the Dublin Boys Club in the studio space of an artist friend in mid-2019. Each meeting lasts a couple of hours and – unlike at the football, darts or any other typical men's space – attendees are encouraged to let down their guard and be vulnerable. After a group meditation, they have a men's circle, where they talk about everything from their relationship with their fathers and friendships to heartbreak and what it means to be a man. After that, they take to the hills for a hike or go for a swim in the sea.

If the group can't meet, conversations move from the meeting room to Zoom or an active WhatsApp group, where support is only ever a message away. Speaking to *The Irish Times*, founder Conor said: 'I often get asked, is it like a men's shed? And yes, I suppose it is, but instead of doing small repair jobs, we're fixing ourselves. We're taking a hammer and a saw to everything we've been taught as men: we can't show weakness, you can't open up to your mates, you can't be indecisive, you can't say you're feeling low because you'll be a buzzkill, and from the salvage, we're constructing a more authentic, sustainable masculinity.'

Since its establishment, the free club has spread across the globe, with meetings taking place in Los Angeles, New York, Limerick and even the Mojave Desert, allowing men to bond outside of mainstream male culture.

Artist Encourages Black Excellence

An African-Canadian artist concerned by rising cases of depression among young people has created a special installation to remind them of their potential and inspire them to greatness. The idea came to 43-year-old Luanga 'Lue' Nuwame, a 'cardboard artist' from Mississauga in Ontario, as he considered the impact of isolation from friends and peers on young people while schools remained closed during the 2020 pandemic.

His two *Reflection of Black Excellence* pieces each feature the faces of 14 heroes of Black history, one focused on globally recognised American icons and the other on lesser-known Black trailblazers from the creator's home country, Canada. In the centre of both, Lue placed a mirror to allow the person engaging with the piece to see themselves reflected among Black leaders, sporting champions, nurses and educators. As a final motivational reminder to the person looking in the mirror, he also added the moving motto 'Love Yourself Always'.

Through the *Reflection of Black Excellence* pieces, which feature abolitionist Harriet Tubman, civil rights leader Martin Luther King, Jr and baseball player Jackie Robinson to name but a few, Luanga explained that he wanted to remind young people that each of these individuals were once 'unsure and scared kids' who had gone on to achieve great things. He said: 'Each name and face reflects the beginning of a larger journey into the soul of historical achievements. That person looking into the centre mirror each day will see him or herself among legends – the best of the best. That person [looking into the mirror] IS the best of the best!'

Also known for his online business, Zelpha Comics, which publishes comic book titles, trading cards, board game concepts and cardboard novelties, the *Reflection of Black Excellence* collectibles were created as a limited run, with only 50 editions of each design available. Every part of each signed and numbered piece was made from raw, 100 per cent recyclable materials and hand cut and sculpted by Lue at his studio in Mississauga. Since their launch during Black History Month in 2021, Lue has sold 34 pieces and the concept continues to help inspire children and young people to see the best in themselves.

Virtual Reality App Helps to Fight Mental Health Issues

A Romanian university has created a virtual reality (VR) product that aims to train the human mind to prevent emotional disorders.

VR-Mind was designed by a team at UBB, Babeş-Bolyai University in Romania in collaboration with augmented and virtual reality specialists, EON Reality. The aim of the app is to promote good mental health and it can also be a tool to help people already experiencing emotional issues like depression and anxiety.

Through a series of VR games, the app assesses and modifies three types of cognitive bias – the systematic errors in thinking that occur when people process and interpret information from the world around them. The biases it addresses relate to those that research has indicated are relevant for depression and anxiety: attentional bias, interpretation bias and memory bias.

The games include identifying a target when it appears in front of them, creating sentences from a selection of words in order to gain points and matching pairs in a memorisation task.

The technology aims to train and/or retrain the mind as a way to prevent psychological issues. The final version of the VR-Mind app was launched in August 2020 and in early 2021 it was made available for psychologists to use alongside their other services to support people struggling with mental health issues.

Its launch has been a success and it is hoped that the app will soon be more widely available for use.

Student Turns Waste Crops into Renewable Energy

An engineering student from the Philippines has created a system that generates clean, renewable energy from ultraviolet (UV) light, using cladding made from waste crops.

The AuREUS system was inspired by the physics that causes the spectacular aurora borealis or Northern Lights, in which invisible high-energy particles such as UV are absorbed by luminescent particles that re-emit them as visible light.

Carvey Ehren Maigue identified that similar luminescent particles could be found in certain fruits and vegetables. By extracting the particles and suspending them in resin, Carvey was able to create a substrate that could be used as cladding for walls or between panes of glass on buildings. This absorbed the invisible UV rays bouncing off other buildings, pavements and architecture and re-emitted it as visible light, reflecting it to the edges of the panels and panes.

Applying the same photovoltaic cells used in traditional solar panels along these edges, the visible light can be captured and converted into electricity. Regulated circuits then process the voltage output and the electricity produced can be stored or used directly.

Unlike standard solar panels, most of which are fitted horizontally to face the sun and rely on visible light to generate power, the AuREUS system can produce electricity even when it is not facing the sun, effectively transforming a building clad on all sides into a vertical solar farm.

As well as addressing the issue of climate change, the system – which was the James Dyson Awards first-ever global sustainability winner – also tackles another issue. By upcycling crops damaged by increasingly frequent and extreme weather events and often left rotting in fields, Carvey's system uses the waste food and provides farmers with a way to monetise their lost crops.

Speaking to architecture and design magazine, *Dezeen*, about the project Carvey said: 'We can show people that adapting sustainability to fight climate change is something that can benefit both the present and the future generation and in doing so, we can rally more people in this fight against climate change.'

Carvey and his team are now working towards sourcing 100 per cent of the particles needed from fruit and vegetables (up from 80 per cent), exploring ways to increase manufacturing capacity and also looking at ways to adapt the technology for solar-powered transport.

Freedom Paddle Feeds 27,000

The 27th of April is a day of celebration for South Africans – Freedom Day. Each year, the country marks the anniversary of the first democratic elections, which were held on 27 April 1994. As the first post-apartheid national elections, anyone was able to vote, regardless of race.

While most South Africans celebrate by enjoying the day off work, one young Hout Bay resident decided to mark Freedom Day 2021 (the 27th Freedom Day) by paddleboarding 27 kilometres (17 miles) for charity. The 19-year-old athlete Kola Cohen pledged to 'Paddle for Love' rather than endurance, joining the famous Freedom Paddle to raise money for a local community farming initiative, Love in a Bowl. The project provides nutritious, organic vegetables to the most vulnerable in Hout Bay, a seaside suburb of Cape Town, delivering weekly community pots to 32 different crèches, soup kitchens and non-governmental organisations (NGOs) in the area. Previously, Kola had volunteered in the initiative's gardens, helping to tend and grow food that could be distributed to Hout Bay's poorest residents.

The paddle route took participants on a round trip from Cape Town to Robben Island – where many political prisoners, including former president Nelson

Mandela, were held during the anti-apartheid struggle. After completing the feat on a prone board using just his arms and body strength to propel him, Kola's fundraising efforts generated enough donations to allow Love in a Bowl to create more than 1,000 community pots and feed 27,000 of the city's most vulnerable people.

Speaking of his challenge, Kola said: 'We live in a beautiful country but there are a lot of problems. We all need to use our productive capacity, in whatever form it's in, to make a positive difference in our community. That's exactly what I'm trying to do.'

Safe Passage for Endangered Sea Lions

A council in New Zealand closed a popular coastal road for a whole month to protect a rare sea lion and her cub, who were found nesting on a local golf course.

Dunedin City Council announced the closure of John Wilson Ocean Drive to vehicles in a Facebook post in January 2021 after the pair were seen regularly crossing the road to get to the beach. The mother sea lion, called Hiriwa – 'silver' in Maori – had initially been spotted alone on the green at Chisholm Links Golf Club, a few days before her pup, named Chisholm after its birthplace, made a noisy entrance into the world. The pair then set up home in a bush near the 13th hole.

With the nearby sea the only source of food, Hiriwa walked 1,000 metres (3,280 feet) a day, crossing the road as she travelled to the beach and back to feed, while the pair nested. The road closure, which was met with approval from local residents, meant that over the course of a month Hiriwa only had to concern herself with avoiding male sea lions rather than people and traffic. Local residents could still walk and ride bicycles in the area, but had to keep any dogs on a lead and remain at least 20 metres (6.5 feet) away from the mammals at all times, so as not to risk an attack.

Dunedin is no stranger to endangered sea lions. The city saw its first recorded breeding in mainland New Zealand since pre-European times in 1993, welcoming three breeding females by 2000. Hiriwa's sighting prompted a joyful response from the golf club on social media, saying: 'We're lucky to have marine mammals on our coastline and we need to share the space with them. This is what makes Dunedin's coastline so unique!'

Road closures to protect wildlife in the area are commonplace, although usually only for a matter of hours or days, with the action to protect Hiriwa and her cub being the longest closure of its kind.

The council noted that New Zealand sea lions are one of the rarest of its species, with only 12,000 left in the world. Local biodiversity rangers said that Chisholm was Hiriwa's seventh pup and celebrated the move to protect them. New Zealand's Department of Conservation said that Hiriwa was believed to be one of 23 breeding females, 18 of which had pups. Next breeding season, they estimate this number will grow to 29 and they expect 20–25 new pups to be born, contributing to the recovery of the species on the mainland coastline.

Animal Shelter Lets Donors Dump on Past Lovers

An ingenious fundraising campaign launched by a Kentucky-based animal shelter raised thousands of pounds for animals in their care when they offered to write the names of donors' ex-lovers in their cat litter trays.

The 'smear campaign' was dreamt up by the team at the Lexington Humane Society, the largest pet adoption centre in Central Kentucky. Launched on social media ahead of Valentine's Day 2021, it requested a minimum donation of $10 from anyone wishing to seek 'retripootion' for heartbreak caused by a past partner, by having their name written in the shelter's cat litter trays. In a Facebook post, the shelter said: 'Our adoptable kitties have your back and will dump all over your ex. Cats can be spiteful creatures, and trust us, they are more than happy to take a #2 on your former #1.'

The shelter shared a picture of the name in situ with all donors before the tagged trays were set out for cats at Lexington Humane Society, so they could 'fart for your broken heart' throughout Valentine's Day. Photos of the results of each donation were also available on request.

The campaign went viral and raised almost $2,000 for the Lexington Humane Society, with hundreds of spurned lovers making sure their exes saw the business end of the shelter's feline residents. In the weeks that followed, the shelter also saw a spike in traffic to its website and increased interest in adoptions – in particular for its perfectly potty-trained pusses!

Rainbow Railroad Helps LGBTQ+ People Escape to Safety

When Sami and Mehraj met, it was love at first sight – but Azerbaijan wasn't safe for a gay couple. They were kicked out of their apartment, feared arrest and torture, and were attacked multiple times. On numerous occasions they tried to leave the country, but each time they were forced to return as they could not get the right visas.

Then in 2019 they contacted Rainbow Railroad, an international charity that is helping LGBTQ+ people living in nations where they are persecuted for their sexuality or gender identity to find a path to a safe, new life. The Canadian charity was inspired by and operates on the same principles as the Underground Railroad, a network of secret routes and safe houses established in the United States during the early to mid-nineteenth century, which were used primarily by enslaved African-Americans to escape into free states and Canada.

Rainbow Railroad responds to requests for help from LGBTQ+ people from across the globe, determining effective routes to safety and working with trusted local contacts. They provide support before people at risk are moved and help to arrange travel logistics. The charity then funds all travel to a safe destination country and support on arrival as well.

Between 2015 and late 2020 Rainbow Railroad helped more than 1,200 people in all and facilitated the evacuation, transportation and resettlement of around 550 individuals like Sami and Mehraj. With the charity's help, in 2019 the pair escaped to Spain. Now finally safe, they can talk openly about getting married and having a family. Rainbow Railroad's mission to help persecuted LGBTQ+ individuals to safety continues.

Mural Celebrates Indigenous Culture in Modern Cities

An environmentally-friendly mural celebrating indigenous culture and the role of its elders is spreading an important message in an inner-city Melbourne suburb. The artwork, located in Collingwood, was painted by Gumbaynggirr artist Aretha Brown. It depicts Aboriginal matriarchs and highlights elders as pillars of their community, while also acknowledging the role of young people and the way indigenous culture exists in modern cities.

The mural was painted using a photocatalytic paint, which absorbs pollutants and transforms carbon dioxide into oxygen and organic matter. While the extent of the environmental impact of the method is still being debated, the link between Aretha's culture and respecting the environment is clear.

Speaking about the project, Aretha said: 'In my mind indigenous rights and environmentalism go hand in hand. For example, making sure that elders and their knowledge is passed down, looking at indigenous histories to explain sustainable methods for our future, looking after the land and only taking what you need. Those kinds of philosophies are very similar.'

As well as being an artist, Aretha is also a vocal advocate for First Nation peoples. In 2017, she was the first female elected as Youth Prime Minister at the National Indigenous Youth Parliament, a model Parliament programme that brought young indigenous people from across Australia together to discuss ideas. Aretha describes herself as being 'amazed' by the platform she had established by the age of 20, but prefers to be considered an artist rather than an activist.

Speaking to *Acclaim* magazine, she said: 'I'm just speaking to people about my experiences in high school and my own experiences as a young Aboriginal person, and I'm just trying to do that any which way how. I've done panels, I've done talks, I do murals and it's just me trying to work out how I can explain the politics that I have in as many ways as possible.'

Underground Car Parks Transformed into Mushroom Farms

Underground car parks were a standard feature in Parisian housing blocks built in the 1960s and 70s, with many even allowing enough space for two cars per apartment. But as new ways to travel around the city have emerged, such as Uber, e-scooters and public bicycles, car ownership has declined, leaving millions of square metres of car parks unused.

In a bid to find innovative ways to use this wasted space, local authorities appealed to the public for ideas and were contacted by urban farmers, Cycloponics. With a company strapline that states 'we farm the underground', they were a perfect match. The dark, moist conditions of underground car parks are ideal for Cycloponics' crops of choice – oyster, shiitake and white button mushrooms – so the company set up farms in three locations, including one car park in La Chapelle that had previously been considered a no-go area once rife with crime.

Alongside mushrooms, they also began cultivating chicory, which can be grown in the dark, and started selling their produce to nearby shops. As well as being a good use of space, the initiative is also having a positive impact on the environment and local community. The decision to use their harvest to supply local businesses has reduced the pollution that would be caused if the food was sold further afield. Furthermore, the team are working with organisations to feed local people in need of support.

Although you might not think there would be 'mush-room' (sorry!) for sharing space among their crops, Cycloponics have supported an organisation that provides 4,000 meals a day to hospital workers and another that delivers 500–1,000 packs of vegetables to people in Paris every single day.

Trans-friendly Language Introduced in Maternity Services

An NHS Trust in the UK has launched gender-inclusive birthing language guidelines into its maternity services. In February 2021, Brighton and Sussex University Hospitals NHS Trust introduced clinical and language guidelines designed to support pregnant trans and non-binary people.

In the guidelines, midwives, doctors and nurses are encouraged to use gender-inclusive phrases such as 'chestfeeding', 'birthing parent' and 'parent' or 'second biological parent' alongside 'breastfeeding', 'mother' and 'father' to be more inclusive of LGBTQ+ service users.

The NHS Trust is believed to be the first in the UK to use gender-inclusive language in its internal communications and meetings, with the guidelines also being applied to one-to-one care when appropriate.

Despite an initial backlash, following incorrect suggestions on social media that the trust was eliminating terms such as 'mother' and 'breastfeeding' rather than simply adding more inclusive words, the move was welcomed by midwives, trans and non-binary parents and LGBTQ+ campaigners.

A policy document published by the trust stated: 'Gender identity can be a source of oppression and health inequality. We are consciously using the words "women" and "people" together to make it clear that we are committed to working on addressing health inequalities for all of those who use our services.'

Eleven-year-old Helps Parents in Need

After learning of a shortage of nappies during the early days of the coronavirus pandemic, 11-year-old Cartier Carey spent the summer holiday at his lemonade stand in Hampton, Virginia, raising money to buy supplies for parents who needed help. In the end, he raised $4,500 – enough to buy more than 22,000 nappies.

When the time came to distribute the goods, on his first day back at school, the driver – a mother herself – shared a surprising story. She told Cartier that his actions reminded her of a time when she'd been in need and someone had helped her, before hugging him and bursting into tears.

In a video shared by Cartier's mum, Britany Stewart, the woman said: 'You are helping so many people. You have no idea. You see this truck? I didn't always have this truck. I lived in a church home. And coming from where I came from and now here, it's because of people like you. People gave me diapers, you know. You're an amazing young man and you can go far.'

The personal revelation spurred Cartier on to continue his good work. He has set up a charity called Kids 4 Change with his mum as a way of encouraging other children to see that they are never too young to make a difference.

Paralysed Extreme Sports Enthusiast Makes Outdoors More Accessible

For most people, being left paralysed at the age of 20 after a devastating snowboarding accident would put an end to participating in extreme sports, but not Christian Bagg.

When six-foot-four Christian broke his back in 1996 he couldn't even find a wheelchair that fitted him properly. But drawing on knowledge garnered from his apprenticeship in machining at the University of Calgary, Christian built his own bespoke chair. He didn't stop there. Realising that he would be dependent on technology for almost everything in his life, he directed his skills towards creating equipment that would enable him to do the things he needed and wanted to do.

Undeterred from participating in high-octane pursuits, Christian tried out equipment that would enable him to get outdoors, but often found it lacking. After taking up cross-country sit-skiing, he found that terrain was often too steep to go up or down and he would run into problems. To address the issue, he came up with an articulating framework, which comprised a parallelogram that allowed him to lean to one side, letting one ski drop low and the other come up high when he hit a side slope.

It was then that he had his eureka moment. If the framework could work on snow, with skis, it could also work on land, with wheels – allowing him to get outside in the summer months. He applied the same concept to a trike he owned, creating a bike that separated the functions of leaning and steering, putting the rider in control. Christian turned his idea into a product and started building the adaptive trikes for others. Having always preferred manual wheelchairs and trikes operated by hand cranks, he never considered creating a motorised version, until a persistent customer persuaded him that he should.

After trying a version of the bike fitted with an electric motor, Christian never went back and that prototype became the foundation for the Bowhead Reach – an adapted electric motorbike powered by a 300-watt electric motor which can also carry a passenger. It can go at 31 m.p.h. into a turn without flipping over and the narrow design means it can even navigate single track trails, allowing the rider to both keep up with others and avoid holding them back by blocking the trail.

The Bowhead Reach retails for around $15,000, but Christian has partnered with a number of foundations which provide grants for people who need assistance purchasing a bike. Twenty-five years after his accident, through sheer ingenuity and tenacity, he isn't only ensuring that he can get out in the great outdoors – he's making sure outdoor exploration remains accessible for all people with disabilities and injuries.

Sweden Builds Reindeer Bridges

With climate change causing warmer weather, Sweden is seeing more frequent rainfall instead of snow, with the former freezing on surfaces. This leaves the country's 250,000 reindeer with a big problem, because the lichens they feed on are being trapped beneath a layer of ice, making them impossible to reach. To find food, the reindeer must travel further afield and this often means crossing busy motorways. In many cases, when herds try to cross these roads they have to be shut down entirely, causing significant disruption.

However, the Swedish transport authorities are building new bridges to help the reindeer. The so-called 'renoducts' – a portmanteau combining the Swedish word for reindeer *ren* and viaduct – will not only allow the reindeer to safely travel to more fertile feeding grounds and reduce the risk of collision between animals and vehicles, but they will also help the 4,500 indigenous Sámi people who herd the animals.

Twelve renoducts are planned initally and Sámi herders have been consulted on their design, so that reindeer are more likely to use them. Their recommendations included two-metre-high (6.5 feet) barriers running along the sides to prevent the animals from falling and that the bridges be uncovered, so the reindeer will not be scared to cross.

Sweden's reindeer viaducts are just one example of a growing number of wildlife crossings around the world. In Mexico, specially-constructed underpasses have been created for jaguars and Christmas Island features bridges that allow red crabs to safely reach beaches during their annual migration, each averting avoidable wildlife deaths.

World's Whitest Paints Could Fight Global Warming

Scientists have created so-called 'ultra-white' paints which reflect so much light that any surface painted with them ends up being cooler than the temperature of the surrounding atmosphere. In October 2020, an ultra-white paint based on calcium carbonate – the mineral that makes chalk – was deemed so reflective that it could be used to keep surfaces and even entire buildings cool.

But in 2021 another team of scientists at Pardue University in Indiana, USA, bettered that attempt by creating a paint using barium sulphate. The alternative formula is estimated to reflect 98.1 per cent of sunlight, a whole 2.6 per cent more than the paint using calcium carbonate as its basis. Using the paint on a surface would mean that only 1.9 per cent of the heat from sunlight would be absorbed.

The team behind the world's whitest paint, whose work was published in the journal *ACS Applied Materials & Interfaces*, have created a game-changer in the battle against global warming. The paint could be used to cool buildings, rather than air conditioners that consume power often derived from burning fossil fuels.

Although not yet available for commercial use, scientists say that modelling has shown that using the paint on between 0.5 and 1 per cent of earth's surface will stop the warming trend. While this is a difficult feat, painting human-made structures could still have a significant impact.

A Hub of Hope for Mental Health

Liverpool comedian and writer Jake Mills suffered with depression and battled internal turmoil for months before his darkest moment proved to be a turning point that would provide hope for thousands of people.

In 2014, Jake started his journey on the road to recovery by posting on social media and speaking publicly about his mental health. His posts and articles were shared with tens of millions by celebrities including actors Emma Watson and James Corden. As his story went viral, he was inundated with messages from people who were struggling too and who had no idea where to turn. It was then that he realised in his darkest hour, neither had he.

He began looking at access to mental health support in the UK and found it fragmented and confusing, with long waiting lists for referrals and local interim help difficult to find. The largest support database that he was able to find comprised just 25 national and London-centric services.

Jake established his own mental health charity, Chasing the Stigma, and decided to collate all the information he could find so that it could be accessed more easily. Recruiting the pro-bono support of a local software development consultancy called Mashbo, in 2017 Jake led the creation of the Hub of Hope, a free mental health support app (www.hubofhope.co.uk).

What started as a spreadsheet listing a handful of helplines is now the UK's most comprehensive mental health support signposting tool. More than 3,000 services are registered and the app is used by organisations including British Transport Police, Mental Health First Aid and Network Rail. In April 2021 the app was included in the UK government's COVID-19 mental health and wellbeing recovery action plan and added to the official NHS.UK website, helping more than 26,533 visitors find support in its first two months on the site.

To date, the app has directed more than 200,000 people to life-changing and even life-saving support and is also the foundation for Chasing the Stigma's accessible mental health training programme, Ambassadors of Hope.

Now the CEO of his own charity, a father of two and a voice for those with lived experience of mental health issues, Jake says: 'I am living proof that you can come back from the brink of suicide. There is always help and there is always hope. We all have mental health, sometimes it's good and sometimes it isn't. It is my mission to make sure people across the UK have

the help they need at their fingertips, whenever they
need it.'

Light Show Transforms
Leek Field

A Dutch designer inspired by science has created a
piece of dazzling light art that improves plants' growth
and resilience using special light 'recipes'.

Experienced in darkness by viewers, the installation
appears as a breathtaking sea of dancing lights washing
across a huge agricultural field. However, Daan
Roosegaarde's artwork, GROW, takes photobiology
light science technologies to a whole new level.

The artist created the luminous dreamscape in a
20,000 square metre (215,300 square feet) leek field in
Lelystad in the Netherlands, painstakingly positioning
thousands of solar-powered LED lights to shine on the
plants at different wavelengths. Special combinations
of red and blue light help the plants to grow faster,
while ultraviolet light boosts their immunity.

The installation was based on scientific research that
shows certain combinations of light or 'light recipes'

can enhance plant growth and reduce the use of pesticides by up to 50 per cent. It was the result of two years of design work by Daan's business, Studio Roosegaarde, and informed by experts from Wageningen University & Research (WUR).

In a video showcasing the mesmerising results, Daan said: 'We often dream about building a better future, yet we hardly notice the fields that feed us. How can we show the beauty of agriculture? How can we make the farmer the hero? And how can light help crops to grow more sustainably?'

With standard lights already commonly used to grow plants in greenhouses and vertical farms, the artwork was intended to inspire farmers to use light more innovatively in agriculture – in particular, encouraging them to consider using more sustainable, solar-powered LED lights. A narrator said: 'GROW is the dreamscape which shows the beauty of light and sustainability. Not as a utopia but as a protopia, improving step by step.'

Daan and his team at Studio Roosegaarde are now aiming to create more installations to show the beauty of combining art and science to create a better world. He intends to take GROW to 40 different countries and provide each local crop with its own unique light recipe to enhance and optimise growth.

Hospital's Rooftop Farm Feeds Boston's Most Vulnerable

A hospital that transformed its rooftop into a fully organic vegetable farm now produces up to 3,175kg (7,000lb) of food a year – improving the health of some of the city's most vulnerable people. The Boston Medical Centre (BMC) in Massachusetts, USA, transformed its rooftop as a way of supporting its Preventative Food Pantry scheme and has since become the largest safety net hospital in New England – one that supports mainly elderly and lower-income patients.

However, its development was not without challenges. Crucially, the hospital roof needed to be strengthened to enable it to hold the amount of soil required to grow the plants and crops, at a cost of $200,000. This was outside of the hospital's budgetary constraints, but a donation from a local philanthropist secured the project's future.

A local green roof specialist called Recover designed and installed the farm, creating an enormous 650 square metres (7,000 square feet) of growing space on the roof. Around 2,400 milk crates were secured to grow the food in and compost-based soil selected as the basis for the farm, with volunteers spending six hours transferring compost-filled crates from a service lift to their new home. Each of the growing crates was also set up to be watered by a hosepipe system that runs separately into each individual crate and turns itself off when rainfall is detected.

The farm now grows 25 different types of vegetable, from spinach and radishes to carrots and peppers. There are also two beehives – which have been painted with honeycomb shapes in bright colours by young patients – inhabited by up to 200,000 resident bees. The bees pollinate 75 per cent of the produce on the farm and make around 68kg (150lb) of honey a year.

Sustainability and education remain core to BMC's use of the farm: it is not only used to produce healthy organic food, but is also a place to teach staff about food's role as medicine. The hospital also has ambitions to expand the farm, so it will be able to feed, nourish and educate local people for many years to come.

Salon Uses Hair to
Clean the Ocean

A salon in Scotland aiming to attract a young, eco-conscious clientele has developed a unique environmentally-friendly technique – using its customers' hair to clean up ravaged oceans and waterways.

After customers have enjoyed a trim at Luvely, in Dalkeith, their hair is saved so that it can be packed into recycled nylon hosiery, covered in mesh and made into 'hair booms' that are used for soaking up coastal oil spills. Once used to absorb the oil, the booms can then be cleaned and used all over again.

The trendy salon, which boasts a graffiti wall and live DJ sessions, operates a strict waste separation policy, with special bins for materials such as used foils, chemicals like leftover colouring products and the crucial hair clippings. The initiative came about after salon owner, Gemma Hill, stumbled across the Green Salon Collective on social media, an organisation that helps hairdressers and beauty salons in the UK to be more sustainable by 'recycling the unrecyclable'.

Amazed by the way the organisation was using hair to clean up local coastlines and waterways, Gemma signed up to the collective immediately, further improving the salon's environmental credentials, which include using products with environmentally-friendly ingredients and participating in schemes that help to remove plastic waste from the ocean.

Priest's Hunger Hunt Project Helps Thousands

On the first day of every month in Kerala, South India, 20,000 packets of food are distributed to care homes and orphanages across the state, thanks to a local priest's ingenious idea.

The Reverend Father Davis Chiramel's 'Hunger Hunt' initiative asks people to donate just 65 rupees – approximately 63 pence or 88 cents – per day to pay for one meal for a person in need. The donations are then used to purchase food. Prison inmates across Kerala help to prepare meals and volunteers from the YMCA manage the logistics of distributing the food to people across the region who are going hungry.

Father Chiramel, an Indian-Catholic priest based in the Archdiocese of Thrissur, had already established food and clothing banks in the towns of

Vadakkanchery, Koratty and Kadangode during the global pandemic in 2020, but aimed to have a more far-reaching impact with his Hunger Hunt project.

The idea was initially met with apprehension, with authorities concerned that the project relied so heavily on a network of volunteers, but it has been a resounding success – something Father Chiramel credits to the work of the volunteers and the generosity of the public, with even lower-income households pitching in what they can afford.

Speaking to the *New Indian Express*, he said: 'People are very generous at heart, and if they find a genuine cause, they won't hesitate to contribute.'

This project is not the first time that Father Chiramel's actions have had a significant impact. In 2009, he earned the nickname 'the kidney priest of Kerala' after he donated a kidney to a man from Vadanapilly in Thrissur who had suffered renal failure. On the day of the operation, he launched the Kidney Federation of India in a bid to promote kidney donation in the country, where organ donation is not yet commonplace due to lack of public awareness and religious or superstitious beliefs. According to reports, this action led to half a million people in India pledging to donate their kidneys after death.

Graphic Novel Gives Voice
to Homeless Young People

When UK-based youth charity Accumulate launched a project to share the stories of people affected by homelessness, it expected to raise awareness and some funds for the charity – it never expected that the project would send one of its contributors to university.

The first-ever graphic novel to be created by people affected by homelessness, *The Book of Homelessness* includes stories about the lives and experiences of contributors, with honest and direct accounts of being forced to leave their homes, countries, relationships, families, the care system and even prison.

Since 2016, Accumulate has helped eight students progress onto degree courses at a university through its scholarship scheme. Profits from the book are added to the scholarship fund, after a share has been distributed among contributors. Within two weeks of the launch of the £25 book, the charity was stunned to realise that the first print run had completely sold out. A second run was printed and the high sales continued, allowing one Accumulate participant to progress their creative education and study, fully funded, on the Access to Higher Education course at Ravensbourne University London, which is designed for people with an interest in design or digital media, who are returning to education.

While raw in their descriptions of pain, abuse, rejection and misplaced love, the tales in the book are also stories of hope, resilience and determination by people who are using their creativity to help change perceptions of homelessness. Comprising drawings, texts, images and poems, *The Book of Homelessness* allowed its contributors to take control of their own stories, while also raising money that was shared between the project's participants and the charity. Thanks to the project's success, the charity continues to provide creative workshops for homeless people.

Wheelchairs Transform 20,000 Costa Rican Lives

It seemed unlikely that Doña Mariana would be able to comfortably celebrate her 106th birthday after falling and fracturing her hip – until the Do It Foundation stepped in to help.

The Costa Rican non-profit organisation was set up in 2005 by the founder of the development company

Grupo Do It, John Scheman. While working to address infrastructure needs in rural schools and local health centres across Guanacaste, he noticed that a significant number of people were living with mobility issues, but could not afford the most basic wheelchair, which came at a cost of around $133.

In response, John established the Do It Foundation with the aim of providing empowerment, hope, mobility and freedom to people with disabilities. The charity aims to ensure that a wheelchair is delivered to every child, teen and adult in Costa Rica who needs one, but cannot afford one.

The wheelchairs are assembled by trained volunteers in Costa Rica and over the last 15 years, the foundation has helped more than 20,000 families throughout Costa Rica and southern Nicaragua.

Speaking to news website *AM Costa Rica* about the anniversary of the scheme, John said: 'It's a blessing of being able to help by giving away something that provides something as essential as independence and mobility, and you can see all the new possibilities in their eyes in a matter of seconds, all the time and effort is worth it.'

Nashville Hotel Changes Lives

A boutique hotel in Nashville, Tennessee, is providing more than just an enjoyable stay for guests in one of the city's most creative districts, it's giving back to its community too.

Renovated from the historic East Nashville Church of Christ, which has provided refuge, safety and a sense of belonging to people in need since 1925, The Gallatin hotel has committed to continuing the legacy of the building's former occupants. The business gives away a substantial proportion of the revenue generated through its accommodation to organisations providing support to homeless people through its Rooms for Rooms program.

The Gallatin is one of three hotels owned by Anchor Rentals that participate in this scheme, with the Russell Hotel and 506 Lofts also giving away a generous chunk of each night's stay and more than 50 per cent of their profits to local ministries and partners helping homeless people in the city, including People Loving Nashville, Room in the Inn, Nashville Rescue Mission and ShowerUp.

A weekend stay can provide up to 16 nights, 100 free showers or 30 free meals for those in need. Over the course of five years, stays at the three properties have provided more than 100,000 hot meals, beds and showers for homeless people in their community and they all continue to invite socially minded guests to 'stay here, change lives'.

Giant Sandcastle Creates Home for Tiny Birds

A giant sandcastle that appeared near a small English town in Surrey was revealed to have a very special purpose – to provide a home for generations of a tiny bird.

The 20-metre-wide (65-feet) and 400-tonne sand installation at Spynes Mere nature reserve near Merstham was unveiled by Surrey Wildlife Trust as a 'nesting bank' for sand martins, tiny 12-centimetre (4.7-inch) brown and white birds that visit the reserve each year as they return from sub-Saharan Africa.

The installation is a vital one as the birds' population has plummeted twice in the last 50 years due to droughts in Africa and a decrease in their nesting habitat in the UK, inland along riverbanks and in quarries.

Sand martins appear at the reserve in mid-March and feed there until September. With their new habitat in place, they will use their tiny claws to dig burrows 50–90 centimetres (20–35 inches) long into the vertical walls and create a small chamber at the end. The sand martins will then peep their heads out of the holes in search of a mate. After mating, they will line the inner chambers with vegetation and feathers and lay between four and eight eggs.

Surrey Wildlife Trust worked with professional sand sculptors, Sand in Your Eye, to create several 1.8-metre (6-foot) test sandcastles to see if the sand held its shape before the project began. The nest bank was created using only sand from the site. Water was added to the sand in a giant bucket mould made from wooden boards. The sand was compacted and left for three to four weeks before the boards were removed.

Described by its creators as a 'des res' (desirable residence) for sand martins, the site now provides 100 square metres (1,076 square feet) of space for their homes. Up to a metre (3 feet) of the sandbanks will be removed annually to tackle nest parasites and after five or six years, the bank will be rebuilt using recycled sand. The birds will be able to move in and sculpt homes for themselves and future generations, while the natural sandbank also becomes a home to solitary bees and wasps. It is hoped that the sand martins will return to the sandcastle year after year to roost together, giving them the security and comfort to allow their population to grow safely.

Chef Finds 'Rice of the Sea' in Ocean Garden

A Michelin-starred chef renowned for creating innovative seafood dishes has cultivated a grain that he believes could change the way we use our oceans.

For almost 15 years Spain's Chef del Mar (Chef of the Sea), Ángel León, has served meals created using produce from the sea that no one else wanted – from discarded fish parts to sea-grown versions of tomatoes and pears – at his restaurant Aponiente in Cádiz. However, a grain that he and his team first encountered in 2017 has led to what Ángel describes as the most important creation of his career.

The team had been working with common eelgrass or *Zostera marina* for some time, when Ángel noticed clusters of grains clinging to the base of the stringy sea plant. Unsure if it was edible, Ángel began researching the marine grain and eventually found a 1973 article in the journal *Science*, which confirmed that it was a staple food for the Seri, an indigenous people living in Mexico.

A pilot project revealed that the grain *Zostera* – dubbed 'the rice of the sea' – could be cultivated in salt water without the need for fertiliser, while lab tests found it to be fibre-rich, gluten-free, high in omega-6 and omega-9 fatty acids and packed with more protein per grain than brown rice. After rigorous testing in Ángel's kitchen, using the grain to mimic popular Spanish rice dishes and make flour for bread and pasta, he discovered that it also tasted good.

Described as being similar to rice or quinoa, but with a saltier taste, *Zostera* is not only healthy, but also good for the environment. The eelgrass is home to many species of marine animals and the meadows are also capable of absorbing CO_2 up to 35 times more efficiently than rainforests do.

In 2021, *Zostera* was approved by the UN as an official grain. Always with his eye on the future of the planet, of the 22,000kg (48,500lb) that Ángel planned to harvest, 19,000kg (41,900lb) was set aside to be used to create new eelgrass farms. He and his team have also created a research and development centre focused on the cultivation of marine vegetation. With three quarters of the planet covered in salt water, they aim to change how we see oceans and think of them as a garden where crops can be grown, while also mitigating the effects of climate change.

Project Gives New Life to Broken Pottery

At the Nozomi Project in Ishinomaki, Japan, an all-female team takes pieces of broken pottery and transforms them into beautiful, unique pieces of jewellery that are sold across the globe. However, there is more to this project than meets the eye. It is based in the Tōhoku region, one of the areas worst affected by the earthquake and tsunami that hit on 11 March 2011. The broken pottery that the company uses to craft its pieces are fragments remaining from the disaster.

With a company motto of 'finding beauty in brokenness', the project draws on the concept of *wabi-sabi*, a worldview centred on the acceptance of imperfection and transience, and the term *mottainai*, which expresses regret over waste as well as remembering those lost in the 2011 disaster.

Nozomi was the brainchild of Sue Takamoto, who moved to the area in 2012 after visiting with aid teams and donations in the wake of the disaster. More than 3,500 lives were lost, 400 people were declared missing and more than 50,000 homes and buildings were destroyed.

While participating in a park clean-up with a group of local mums who had helped her settle into the area, Sue noticed countless pieces of broken pottery lying under destroyed vehicles and piles of dead fish that had been washed inland by the tsunami. Speaking to *Japan Times*, she said: 'It seemed like such a waste, so I started collecting it.'

Together, Sue and her friends set about learning how to make jewellery from the pieces, cutting them, shaping them with grinding tools and mounting them to create necklaces, earrings, rings, bracelets and other accessories. As their skills developed, Sue spotted an opportunity to provide work for women in the area, after seeing local unemployment rise by more than 300 per cent, with women disproportionally affected. Shortly afterwards, the business was formally established and a number of jewellery styles were created, each named after a team member's loved one – daughters, mothers and others lost in the tsunami.

The business became not only an economic lifeline to many, but also a source of practical and emotional support, which continues to this day. The company now has 12 members of staff and continues to create memories, hope and joy using pieces from the disaster, as well as pieces donated from pottery damaged in the aftershocks experienced ten years later in 2021. Sue and her team are now planning to extend the opportunity to work with the Nozomi Project to other women around the world, starting with a partnership with a women's centre in Cambodia.

'No Wash Club' Saves Water – and the Planet

A small-batch denim brand based in a town in West Wales is challenging its customers to wait at least six months to wash their jeans in a bid to save the planet.

It sounds crazy, but it's a simple way to get the best out of your jeans and help to protect the environment. Cardigan-based Hiut Denim Co.'s 'No Wash Club' was established to highlight the fact that the longer you leave a new pair of jeans without washing them, the more beautiful and unique-to-you the garment will be. But it also advocates the benefit to what it describes as the company's silent shareholder – Planet Earth.

By encouraging less washing, the company helps to cut energy and water wastage and reduce the carbon footprint created by our washing habits. As well as its No Wash Club, Hiut Denim Co. also adopts innovative technology to help keep jeans fresh and promote the environmentally responsible aftercare of their products.

In 2021, it worked with Swedish chemicals company Polygiene to apply OdorCrunch technology to its 'A-B commuter jeans' at the finishing stage of production. This consists of filtered river water and modified silica sand particles, which break down odours and permanently eliminate them from fabric.

The brand is well-known for being environmentally and socially conscious, with a heart-warming story at the heart of its establishment. In 2002, 400 people were made redundant when the UK's biggest jeans factory, located in Cardigan, closed down. In the 4,000-person town, 400 had been employed at the factory, which had made 35,000 pairs of jeans a week for three decades.

The factory may have relocated, but the skill and knowhow remained, so in 2011 when Hiut cofounder David Hieatt, who had worked in the markets of the

Welsh valleys, was looking for somewhere to manufacture his new brand of jeans, he knew exactly where to go.

Today, the factory makes 12,000 pairs of jeans each year and products sewn by its 'Grand Masters' have even been worn by Meghan, Duchess of Sussex. The royal seal of approval in 2018 prompted a three-month waiting list for its black jeans and a factory move to meet demand.

Expedition Discovers 3,400-year-old Egyptian City

A team hunting for Tutankhamun's mortuary temple near Luxor inadvertently uncovered one of the most important archaeological discoveries since the 1920s. The 3,400-year-old city, The Rise of Aten, was uncovered near the Valley of the Kings, where King Tut's tomb was discovered in 1922. Believed to be a significant industrial and administrative hub during the reign of King Amenhotep III from about 1391 to 1353 BCE, the find provides a glimpse into the day-to-day life of the ancient Egyptians during a time when the country was at the peak of its international power. Previous expeditions to the area had looked for the lost city, but never succeeded.

As the excavations began, archaeologists were stunned to find almost complete walls and rooms filled with artefacts, including scarab rings, wine pitchers and mud bricks bearing the seals of King Amenhotep III's cartouche – the hieroglyphic symbol of an ancient Egyptian pharaoh. Exploring the site room by room, the team also discovered pottery in huge quantities.

Some discoveries were used to establish when the city was active, such as a container found packed with 10 kilos (22lb) of meat, bearing the inscription: 'Year 37, dressed meat for the third Heb Sed festival from the slaughterhouse of the stockyard of Kha made by the butcher Luwy'.

During the first seven months of the excavation, a bakery, food preparation area and large kitchen were found in the southern area of the city. Ovens, kilns and huge quantities of stamped bricks have been found in what is believed to be The Rise of Aten's industrial area, along with tools possibly used for spinning and weaving and evidence of metal and glassmaking. Another partially explored section appears to be its administrative and residential district, boasting bigger and more organised living spaces.

The full excavation is expected to take five years to complete and archaeologists hope to explain the unusual burial of what is believed to be a bull or a cow in a room and reveal the secrets of a collection of yet-to-be explored tombs.

Ecologists Create Fish Doorbell

When fish swim through the canals of Utrecht in spring, how do they pass through the Netherlands city's closed Weerdsluis lock gate? Using a doorbell, of course!

Fish play an important role in keeping Utrecht's rivers and canals healthy and clean. Each spring, thousands of fish pass through its canals towards the Weerdsluis lock – where the city meets the River Vecht – in search of a place to lay their eggs. Unfortunately, the Weerdsluis lock doesn't open very often at this time of year and 'fish jams' frequently occur. Travelling closer to the surface in spring as they seek to reproduce, the fish are exposed and the longer they have to wait at the unopened lock, the more likely they are to be eaten by other animals, such as grebes and cormorants.

While working on a project to highlight the biodiversity of Utrecht's canals, fish expert Mark van Heukelumand and wildlife ecologist Anne Nijs looked at ways to address the problem. Keen to ensure safe passage for the canals' travellers, they came up with a very unexpected solution.

After watching the lock operator opening the gate to let some fish through, they decided to set up an underwater camera at the lock and livestream footage to a homepage containing a digital 'fish doorbell'. If local residents or visitors saw fish waiting to pass, they could press the doorbell and alert the lock operator to the waiting fish, so that the gates could be opened for them. A total of 440,000 people rang the fish doorbell in 2021, securing its return for future spring breeding seasons. You can go to https://visdeurbel.nl/ to watch the livestream when it next goes live.

When asked if installing a motion-activated sensor might have been more convenient, Anne explained that their approach was a great way to connect residents to their aquatic neighbours, while Mark lauded the fish doorbell solution as simply being 'much more fun'.

Scientists Create Single-use Plastic That 'Eats Itself'

As more people have become aware of the scourge of single-use plastics, they have turned to biodegradable plastics as a solution to the plastic pollution problem. But recyclers and scientists have been faced with a challenge. Many of these compostable plastics don't break down during typical composting processes, so still end up in landfill and last as long as standard single-use plastics.

Thankfully, a team at University of California, Berkeley believe they have come up with a solution – a single-use plastic that 'eats itself'. Working with compostable plastics made primarily of the polyester known as polylactic acid (PLA), the research involved embedding inexpensive and readily available polyester-eating enzymes in the plastic as it's made.

The enzymes were protected by a simple polymer wrapping, which it would 'shrug off' once exposed to heat and water. The enzyme then starts breaking down the plastic polymer into its building blocks. For PLA, this means reducing it to lactic acid, which can feed the soil microbes in compost. The polymer wrap degrades and the process also eliminates microplastics, a by-product of many chemical degradation processes and a pollutant in its own right.

The study found that to trigger degradation, it was necessary only to add water and a little heat. At room temperature, 80 per cent of the modified PLA fibres degraded entirely within about one week, with the plastic breaking down faster at higher temperatures.

Ting Xu, UC Berkeley professor and senior author of the paper on the process, written for the journal *Nature*, believes that the new technology should theoretically be applicable to other types of polyester plastics, perhaps allowing the creation of compostable plastic containers, which currently are made of polyethylene, a type of polyolefin that does not degrade.

In a release from UC Berkeley, Ting said that the process could be the key to recycling many objects: 'Imagine using biodegradable glue to assemble computer circuits or even entire phones or electronics, then, when you're done with them, dissolving the glue so that the devices fall apart and all the pieces can be reused.

'It is good for millennials to think about this and start a conversation that will change the way we interface with earth. Look at all the wasted stuff we throw away: clothing, shoes, electronics like cellphones and computers. We are taking things from the earth at a faster rate than we can return them. Don't go back to earth to mine for these materials, but mine whatever you have, and then convert it into something else.'

Homophobic Slurs Raise Funds for LGBTQ+ Organisations

A Lithuanian artist has taken 400 homophobic slurs posted online and used them to raise thousands of pounds for organisations supporting LGBTQ+ people. Erikas Malisauskas collated hundreds of abusive messages directed at Tomas Raskevicius – the first LGBTQ+ activist to be elected to the Lithuanian parliament – and used them to create a digital artwork called *Hate Speech Cloud*.

LGBTQ+ ally Erikas was prompted to create the work after being shocked by the abuse hurled at Tomas and the wider LGBTQ+ community and used his personal skills to find a unique way to show support for the community. Speaking about his work on

Reddit, he explained that he chose to create the black and white image in the shape of a cloud because he believed that 'every cloud in the sky clears away sooner or later' in the same way that he hopes 'the hatred will also clear away'.

His motivation for the piece was to turn the words of homophobic bullies against them, by monetising them and donating the proceeds to LGBTQ+ charities and organisations. He succeeded in his mission when an anonymous buyer purchased the work, raising more than £4,000. An image of the artwork can be viewed at www.neapykantosdebesis.lt

Couple Move into 3D-printed House

At first glance, the Eindhoven home of Elize Lutz and Harrie Dekkers is contemporary and unassuming. Shaped like a large boulder designed to fit in with the natural location, the untrained eye would never detect its secret – it was built using a 3D printer.

The building was Europe's first ever fully 3D-printed house, one of five planned for the site in the Dutch city, as part of Project Milestone – a joint construction and innovation project. The decision to shape the detached, single-storey house like an irregular boulder was both a nod to the local environment and a demonstration of the freedom provided by 3D concrete printing. The house was constructed from 24 individually printed concrete parts, which were printed layer by layer at a local factory. Each part was then transported to the site and placed on a foundation, after which the building was given a roof and frames.

Inside, it appears like any other home, with two beautifully decorated bedrooms and a living area spread across 94 square metres (1,011 square feet). Its thick insulation and connection to a heat grid make it incredibly energy efficient and despite being printed piece by piece, it meets all strict Dutch building requirements.

The technique represents a huge opportunity for sustainable and affordable home design, as well as offering the potential for more flexible and personalised designs. Printed homes are also, in principle, faster to construct than traditional buildings.

Speaking of Project Milestone, Yasin Torunoglu from the Municipality of Eindhoven said: 'Innovation is an important pillar in construction. In addition to affordable homes, the market increasingly demands innovative housing concepts.

'With the 3D-printed home, we're now setting the tone for the future: the rapid realisation of affordable homes with control over the shape of your own house … I'm proud that this promising innovation has a place in our city.'

The project's ultimate ambition is to make 3D concrete printing a sustainable method of construction that will pave the way for more affordable housing. As each of the five planned houses is built, it will inform the building of the next and will enable the team behind the project to develop the technique and allow it to create multi-storey houses.

Front Lawn Microfarms Feed Whole Community

A Los Angeles-based start-up is transforming everyday lawns into microfarms that provide whole neighbourhoods with ultra-local produce – and homeowners with a share of the profits.

Crop Swap LA teams up with homeowners who have a front garden and a desire to make a positive impact on their local area and environment. The company installs its Asante Microfarms – *asante* means 'thank you' in Swahili – and maintains the plot, while its homeowners receive a monthly share of the produce *and* profit from sales of its harvest, which is sold as a monthly subscription to residents living within a few miles of the farm. Ten per cent of the harvest is also donated to the community in areas most affected by food insecurity.

Each microfarm grows more than 600 organically-grown vegetables and plants and can feed up to 50 families. It captures and recycles water and also stores more than 3,000 litres (3,170 quarts) that can be used to grow even more food, including kale, rainbow chard and tomatoes.

The techniques used to farm the plots use just eight per cent of the water that would previously have been used to grow and maintain a lawn and local people can get three pounds of fresh, organic vegetables and greens for just $36 per month.

Determined to grow food in any unused spaces, in 2021 Crop Swap LA launched its wall gardens, which grow 36 types of lettuces, herbs and vegetables and can be installed on balconies, walkways, apartment buildings and in commercial spaces.

Jamiah Hargins, who founded the business in 2018, eventually hopes to help build and manage 400 microfarms across LA.

Graffiti Artists Create Colouring Book to Stimulate Kids' Creativity

A collaborative colouring book created by graffiti and street artists from around the globe is encouraging kids' creativity.

The Smiles 4 Miles project was started by London graffiti artist Pixie, who collected drawings donated by her peers to create a colouring book for kids, selling the first edition online and at markets, where she and her pals dressed as colourful crayons to attract buyers' attention. All of the profits – along with more colouring books – were donated to the Refugee Children's Bus Project and the Hummingbird Project, which provide educational activities for refugee children.

The project has been so popular that in 2020 Pixie decide to launch a second edition and attempt to transform a great idea into a self-sustaining project that would raise money for the Teapot Trust, an organisation that offers art therapy to children coping with chronic illnesses.

Pixie once again collected drawings from fellow street and graffiti artists, this time launching a public vote to decide which images would be included in the next book. The winning artists came from all over the world, including Germany, the UK, the USA, Australia and New Zealand. Alongside the drawings were contributions from the artists, ranging from poetry and art tips to funny stories and words of encouragement.

Liverpool-based artist Charlie Weatherstone or Luna, whose illustration about connecting with people and mental health was reflected in her character's flowing locks, wrote: 'Reading feeds your brain with knowledge, interesting words and ideas that formulate curious characters, just like my swirly-haired Luna ladies in the book.

'Listen to others, always look forward, onward and upwards, and don't be afraid to ask for help. Be yourself, be kind to yourself, be kind to nature and be kind to others. And finally, have fun and don't forget to enjoy a big piece of cake from time to time – you'll deserve one when you have finished colouring in this magnificent book.'

Although a Kickstarter project launched in 2021 didn't quite hit its target, many of those who backed the idea went on to donate and purchase the book from the Smiles 4 Miles website, or commission the featured artists who were able to donate the proceeds to the Teapot Trust. Boosted by the support, Pixie, who is now focused on creating illustrations and paintings for children, has transformed her idea into a not-for-profit initiative. Every time a colouring book is purchased from smiles4milesbooks.com, the organisation prints another one to give to a child who needs it, starting with those in children's hospitals, and it also donates £4 to the Teapot Trust.

Researchers Create Pineapple Leaf Drones

A team of researchers from University Putra Malaysia (UPM) have created a lightweight drone that can be built out of pineapple leaves. Despite their unusual construction material, the drones are exceptionally durable, with a higher strength-to-weight ratio than traditional, synthetic ones, and can be flown up to 1,000 metres (3,280 feet) for up to 20 minutes.

It is hoped that the design will eventually be used to create drones suitable for agricultural imaging, which can help farmers quickly detect and respond to seasonal problems that might impact their land and yield.

The research team, led by Professor Mohamed Thariq Hameed Sultan, has been exploring this ingenious use of pineapple leaves, which are often burned or thrown away by Malaysian farmers after the fruit has been harvested, since 2017. However, it is only now that their idea has taken flight.

Drones made from waste pineapple leaves are durable and also cheaper to produce than other drones, as well as using less power to fly because they are light in weight. What's more, the innovation provides an environmentally friendly and sustainable alternative to synthetic drones. Preventing farmers from burning the leaves in the first place reduces damage to the environment, and if the drone malfunctions, it can easily be fixed using the abundance of pineapple leaves available. The broken part can then simply be buried in the ground and left for two weeks to decompose.

The team is now working on making larger versions of the drone that can carry more weight. It has ambitions to ensure that the project improves the livelihood of farmers both through the provision of technology and the scaling up of manufacture, which would provide an additional source of revenue for farmers wishing to sell their waste pineapple leaves, rather than burning them.

Botanist Teaches the Value of Weeds

A botanical campaign in London is helping to change perceptions about some of our most unloved plants, with supporters chalking the names of weeds onto urban pavements and walls.

Inspired by an initiative created in France called *sauvages de ma rue* or 'wild things of my street', London-based French botanist Sophie Leguil launched the More Than Weeds campaign in the UK in 2019 as a way of encouraging people to learn about the plant life that inhabits our cities.

In a video promoting the French campaign that has garnered more than seven million views, Boris Presseq, a botanist at the Toulouse Museum of Natural History, walks around his city chalking the names of the plants he finds on pavements and walls as a way of highlighting their presence, promoting knowledge of the area's biodiversity and encouraging respect for wild plants.

While Sophie doesn't encourage the trend for 'botanical chalking' employed by rebel botanists like Boris – it is illegal to write in chalk on any public pavement in the UK without permission – she highlights it as a cheap and effective way in which local councils could educate residents about the plants poking up between paving stones and their place in the urban ecosystem.

Through the More Than Weeds Twitter account, which now has almost 10,000 followers, Sophie shares pictures of plants in urban environments, encourages followers to do the same and helps them to identify them. She also delivers talks on the topic and works with individuals and organisations on nature and conservation projects.

In France the 'wild things of my street' project has already been a huge success. Since 2011, more than 100,000 records of wild plants have been contributed by local groups, covering 340 species and data collected by the project has been used by scientists for research on urban species richness, pollination ecology and climate change. Some councils have even encouraged residents to sow native wild plants in pavement cracks and along walls.

Sophie has similar hopes for the UK initiative, with ambitions to encourage the recording of urban flora through guided walks, social media and the publication of identification guides, as well as encouraging local authorities to 'embrace urban biodiversity and learn how to live with plants growing on pavements, gutters, on walls or in tree pits'.

As well as being a joyful initiative, protecting our most unloved plants and encouraging their growth in cities and towns can also have a huge impact on the local environment, with many species of plant considered common weeds providing more pollen per flower than other, wilder species.

Area of Forest the Size of France Regrows

An area of forest the size of France has regrown since the year 2000, providing a positive reminder that nature can bounce back, if it is allowed and supported to.

An increasingly rare piece of good news for forests around the globe, the data from a study by Trillion Trees – a collaboration between the World Wide Fund for Nature (WWF), BirdLife International and the Wildlife Conservation Society (WCS) – revealed that 58.9 million hectares (227,414 square miles) of forest had regrown, in locations including the Atlantic Forest in Brazil, northern Mongolia, central Africa and Canada. It also revealed that the area of regrowth could collectively store the equivalent of 5.9 gigatonnes of carbon dioxide – more than the annual emissions of the US.

The study examined more than 30 years' worth of satellite imaging data. Surveying experts with local knowledge of more than 100 sites in 29 different countries created a map of regeneration hotspots which aims to inform forest restoration plans worldwide. The resurgences were revealed to be the result of a variety of factors, including better forest management, government policies, responsible industry practices and migration towards cities, as well as natural occurrences, such as regeneration after forest fires.

The good news was tempered by a warning and a call to act on this glimmer of hope for our forests from William Baldwin-Cantello, Director of Nature-based Solutions at WWF and part of the Trillion Trees project. He said: 'We've known for a long time that natural forest regeneration is often cheaper, richer in carbon and better for biodiversity than actively planted forests, and this research tells us where and why regeneration is happening, and how we can recreate those conditions elsewhere.

'But we can't take this regeneration for granted – deforestation still claims millions of hectares every year, vastly more than is regenerated. To realise the potential of forests as a climate solution, we need support for regeneration in climate delivery plans and must tackle the drivers of deforestation.'

The Trillion Trees project aims to have regrown, saved from loss and improved protection of a trillion trees around the world by 2050, by ending deforestation and advancing restoration. It enables people and programmes to grow the right trees in the right places and ensures healthy and resilient landscapes that support people and nature.

New App Detects Autism
in Toddlers

Using eye-tracking technology to diagnose symptoms of autism spectrum disorder (ASD) isn't new, but making it accessible to everyone is. Research has shown that babies and toddlers who pay more attention to objects than people are more likely to develop ASD and technology that tracks their gaze has been used by professionals to detect this for some time.

But Duke University in North Carolina has developed a tool that could put this technology in the hands of parents and those working with young children through a smartphone app. The app displays short video clips that can be shown to a toddler; these feature a person playing with a toy such as a spinning top, with the toy always on one side and the person on the other. The app tracks the child's gaze and determines its overall direction, helping to detect behaviours linked to ASD.

Tests on around 1,000 toddlers with an average age of 21 months have demonstrated promising results and the team is now undertaking further tests and refining the app before it can be made widely available.

By removing barriers such as access to medical resources, healthcare and the affordability of professional therapeutic tools, the app could allow parents to address their children's needs earlier and educate themselves on how best to support them.

Satellites P-P-P-Pick Up Rare Penguin Poo and Reveal New Colonies

New Emperor penguin breeding sites have been located in the Antarctic, thanks to satellites spotting stains left by the birds' droppings. Large patches of sea ice stained by penguin poo or 'guano' were identified in 2020 by the European Union's *Sentinel-2* spacecraft, which was used by the British Antarctic Survey (BAS) to search for the endangered species.

The evidence suggests that there could be as many as 278,500 breeding pairs across 11 sites, taking the number of known active breeding sites from 50 to 61 and potentially increasing the global population of the birds by as much as ten per cent. Researchers identified the breeding sites using infrared technology and were able to estimate the numbers in the colonies by the size of the bird huddles on the sea ice.

There was more good news for Antarctic wildlife the following year. Researchers in New Zealand studying Antarctic blue whales migrating through the Pacific Ocean estimated that the mammals' numbers in the area had recovered to about three per cent of their pre-exploitation numbers – about 10,000 whales. Antarctic blue whales have been a protected species for 55 years, before which they had been hunted so frequently, less than one per cent of their former population remained.

While the resurgence of both species is small in comparison to previous populations and their natural habitats face continuing challenges, the findings by researchers offer hope for these majestic creatures.

Mini Mermaids Club Empowers Girls

When Hannah Corne's daughter developed selective mutism, a severe anxiety disorder that makes it difficult for her to interact with other people verbally, she began researching anything that could possibly help her manage the condition.

Watching her daughter in different scenarios, Hannah noticed that when she was outside, playing and being active or riding her bike, her anxiety decreased and she was able to interact more comfortably with other children and adults.

She delved further into the relationship between physical activity and other areas of wellbeing, like self-esteem, confidence and self-compassion, and began seeking out clubs or activities that considered the whole child and combined getting young girls moving outdoors with positive mental wellbeing. Unable to find anything that ticked all the boxes in the UK, she stumbled across an American organisation called Mini Mermaids. What first appeared to be just a running club for young girls was in fact so much more. Its programme centres on two characters, Mini Mermaid and Siren, created to represent the two voices we hear in our own heads and out in the world. Mini Mermaid represents the girls' inner cheerleader, while Siren – named after the mythical creatures whose enchanting singing would lure sailors to shipwreck on dangerous rocks – is their inner critic.

Alongside physical activity, the programme teaches the girls to recognise these voices and be able to tell the difference between them. Through mindfulness approaches, club members turn the Mini Mermaids' voice into a powerful one, able to challenge negative self-talk and the pressures they face in the outside world.

Hannah set up the UK's first Mini Mermaid Running Club at a local school in Leeds, Yorkshire, bringing running and workouts together with discussions, games and journalling activities. Key to this is helping the girls to address Siren's negative thoughts with positive Mini Mermaid responses. As well as supporting her daughter's progress, she wanted to create a generation of girls who enjoyed being physically active and had tools to develop a strong sense of self-worth and self-belief that they could carry with them.

Since launching the club, more than 1,500 girls aged seven have joined 11 branches throughout the UK and Ireland and had a 'fintastic' experience, with 80 per cent both enjoying moving their bodies and believing that they are good at things. Hannah is now on a mission to activate Mini Mermaids in every single primary school in the UK.

Spaniard Harnesses the Power of Conversation

You might think that people would give wide berth to a young man sitting on the street in Barcelona, Spain, with two folding chairs and a large handwritten sign offering 'free conversations'. But over the past four years more than 1,400 people have pulled up the empty chair facing 26-year-old Adrià Ballester and accepted the invitation to have an old-fashioned face-to-face chat.

Adrià started offering free conversations after a chance meeting on the outskirts of Barcelona. After a bad day at work, he decided to go for a walk before going home. While wandering the city, he met an 80-year-old man. The pair started talking and Adrià shared his problems with him. After speaking for 30 minutes, just before they parted, the man said: 'When you're 80 years old, all those problems that seem so big now will look so small.'

It was a lightbulb moment for Adrià. He was right. In just a few short minutes, a stranger had provided him with a completely different perspective on his worries.

Afterwards, Adrià realised how people struggled to communicate in this way and became concerned about how disconnected and isolated they were becoming, glued to computers and smartphones instead of speaking and sharing ideas. He recognised the positive impact of speaking openly, outside in the fresh air, and decided to offer the same opportunity to others, taking his two folding chairs and makeshift free conversations sign into the centre of Barcelona.

At first, people were wary and some mocked him, but then they began to join him. Some of the conversations were simple, reflecting on the moment or engaging in general chit-chat, while others were deeper, as people opened up and talked about their problems, heartbreak and past. On many occasions Adrià or his guest would find themselves moved to tears.

Far from being against technology, Adrià simply believes that there is a power in face-to-face conversations that does not exist in tech-based chat, an emotional connection borne from the fact that speaking in person is 'meeting the real character of the story and they are sitting there in front of your eyes'.

Adrià set up a Facebook page (Free Conversations Movement) and an Instagram account (@freeconversations) and, with permission, posted photos of the people he'd spoken to alongside snippets from their conversations. Soon after, people began following his lead, setting up folding chairs in the streets of Taiwan, Mexico, Poland, Dublin and Portugal, to name a few.

The Free Conversations Movement continues to grow, connecting people, promoting the free flow of ideas and moving towards its aim of providing a space in every city where people can freely express themselves.

Gran's LEGO Ramps Make Towns More Accessible

A German grandmother who struggled to access her local shops in her wheelchair has developed a colourful solution – creating ramps made out of LEGO bricks.

Rita Ebel came up with the fun and functional idea from her home in Hanau in Hesse, Germany, after finding it difficult to get into local shops and cafes. Each ramp contains several hundred donated LEGO bricks, stuck together with up to eight tubes of glue.

The concept was embraced by local businesses, who were not only pleased to make their establishments more accessible but also noted the delight the rainbow ramps brought to other customers as well.

Rita, who has used a wheelchair since a car accident 25 years ago, now spends two or three hours a day making the ramps to order, with the help of her husband, Wolfgang. The impact of her idea has spread globally – she has sent ramp-building instructions to Austria and Switzerland, and has even had interest from people in Spain and the US.

It's not the first time LEGO has been used in an innovative way to improve people's lives. In 2020 the company launched LEGO® Braille Bricks, which teach Braille to children who are blind or visually impaired. The bricks, which are currently available in 20 countries and multiple languages, are the same shape as normal LEGO bricks, but their studs are arranged to correspond to numbers and letters in the Braille alphabet. There is also a printed version of the symbol or letter on each brick, so sighted and blind children can play and learn together.

The company also provided a new way for people to de-stress in early 2021, when it launched a playlist called LEGO® White Noise, which features tracks composed using the various sounds made by its iconic bricks. Its designers experimented with over 10,000 sounds to find the most soothing sounds, resulting in tracks including 'It All Clicks' based on 'the joyous sound of two LEGO elements joining together' and

'The Waterfall', which was created by pouring thousands of LEGO bricks on top of one another.

Researchers Uncover Corsica's Mysterious 'Cat-fox'

A mysterious wild animal that gained semi-mythical status in northern Corsica has been identified as a brand-new species. Measuring up to 90cm (35 inches) from its head to the tip of its tail, the *ghjattu volpe* or 'cat-fox' is significantly larger than most domestic cats and has distinctive black striped paws and a black-ringed tail.

Despite rarely being seen due to its nocturnal habits, the cat-fox had been considered a scourge by shepherds on the Mediterranean island, who believed it attacked their flocks. Cat-foxes had largely disappeared into folklore until one was found in a chicken coop in 2008. The catch prompted new research into ways to attract the rare cat so it could be studied properly for the first time. Initially researchers used scented posts for the cats to rub themselves against, so the fur left behind could be used for genetic analysis. But the real breakthrough came in 2016, when a cat-fox was captured and scientists were finally able to study the animal up close. The animal's thick russet-coloured fur is thought to protect it from ticks and fleas, while scientists also noted its wide-set ears, shorter whiskers and larger canine teeth.

While examination of the creature's DNA showed it to be close to the African forest cat, it was not the same. In 2019, after examining and releasing 12 of 16 known cat-foxes over a three-year period, scientists confirmed that they believed it to be a completely new species.

The team, from France's national hunting and wildlife office (ONCFS), called the outcome of the research a 'wonderful discovery' and are now working towards having the cat-fox recognised and protected.

Donkey-dug Wells Help Desert Wildlife Survive

After many years of being overlooked in terms of scientific and ecological importance, the humble donkey has been hailed a vital part of our deserts' ecosystems.

A study published in the journal *Science* has revealed that wells dug by donkeys and horses in desert sands provide an important source of water. Biologist Erick Lundgren, lead author of the paper, turned his attention to the behaviour of desert horses and donkeys after reading about how African elephants dug wells that were the only source of water for other animals during the dry season.

Keen to find out if donkeys and horses had a similar impact in North America, he and his team examined sites in the Sonoran Desert in Arizona and California. They set up cameras to identify which species utilised the hoof-dug wells and looked at the water provided by those wells in comparison to the surface water that was available from permanent and intermittent desert streams.

The research found that the wells dug by donkeys and horses, which reached up to two metres (6.5 feet) in depth, increased water availability for many native desert species including mule deer, bobcats, peccaries and even black bears. During the driest parts of summer, they also reduced the distance between vital water sources and in some cases were the only water source available. As well as providing a water source for native wildlife, the team also observed some river tree species sprouting from abandoned wells, suggesting that they could also act as plant nurseries.

This study is particularly intriguing considering that donkeys and horses, as non-native species, are often studied as 'invasion biology' in relation to damage to the desert ecosystem. Despite being introduced to the continent by Europeans and not being considered local wildlife, it appears that horses and donkeys have been doing their bit to keep water available and acting as buffers to the variability of desert streams due to climate change and human activity.

Plantable Pencils Turn Stubs into Sprouts

An environmentally friendly start-up in the Philippines has launched a pencil that can be planted after use. The product was developed by Eco Hub Cebu as an alternative to throwing away old pencils. Instead of putting an eraser on their pencils, the company added gelatine capsules filled with non-genetically modified plant seeds, meaning they could be planted once they were too short to use for writing or drawing.

The plantable pencil stubs need to be buried in moist soil to grow and can sprout as quickly as five or ten days. The pencils contain many different seed varieties, including basil, chilli pepper, sunflower and tomato.

Staying true to the company's eco-friendly credentials, the pencils are also lead-free and made from sustainable wood, graphite and clay, as well as being preservative and allergen-free. But the pencils are just one part of the company's collection, which aims to make sustainable products more affordable. The company also sells bicycles, kitchen utensils, reusable straws and bamboo toothbrushes.

At present, Eco Hub Cebu assemble the pencils using products sourced from abroad, but the company aims to find a local community to partner with so they can make the pencils locally and provide more job opportunities.

The original idea for the plantable pencil came when three students from the Massachusetts Institute of Technology (MIT) in Boston also added dissolvable seed pods to pencils in response to a brief challenging them to 'design the sustainable office article of tomorrow'. The project eventually grew into the company Sprout World, which extended the same idea to include eyeliner pencils as well.

Teenagers Design App for Dementia Patients

Three teenage girls from Drogheda in Ireland have designed an app to support dementia patients, their families and caregivers. The Memory Haven app was created by Nigerian-Irish teenagers Joy Njekwe, Margaret Akano and Rachael Akano for a competition at the 2020 Technovation World Summit.

The trio were inspired to develop an app to support those affected by dementia after the death of one of their grandmothers, Madam Elizabeth Bello, and the painful experience of watching her 'deteriorate and become a shadow of her old self' as a result of the condition.

The young women identified three key areas that people living with dementia face difficulty with – memory, recognition and speech – and designed an app with features that addressed these issues. The features include a central database of contact details in case of emergency, a reminder feature for appointments and medication schedules, a photo gallery and puzzles to improve cognitive skills, which can help to delay the effects of dementia. The app also offers face and voice recognition tools, both to help patients recognise their family and friends and to allow the app to recognise

their mood, triggering certain responses such as playing upbeat music if sadness is detected.

Their innovation took first place in the Girls Competition at the Technovation World Summit, beating 1,500 entrants from 62 countries. The girls aim to eventually launch the app in the US and more European countries and plan to add further features requested during testing, such as fingerprint recognition technology and a memory game personalised with a user's own images.

Mutant Enzyme Could Transform Plastic Recycling

Scientists at French company, Caribos, have engineered a mutant enzyme that breaks plastic bottles down into their chemical building blocks, ready to be made into new products in a matter of hours.

The work began with the screening of 100,000 microorganisms, from which a base enzyme originally discovered in leaf compost by researchers at Osaka University was selected as the best option. The scientists then introduced mutations that improved its ability to break down polyethylene terephthalate or PET plastic.

PET is the most commonly used polyester plastic, with almost 70 million tonnes manufactured annually around the world, because it is both strong and lightweight. However, current PET recycling only allows clear plastics to be recycled and used to create new, lower-quality products, with coloured or soiled plastics difficult or impossible to recycle and ending up in landfill or being incinerated.

The team eventually optimised the enzyme to be able to break down a tonne of waste bottles, which were 90 per cent degraded in just ten hours. Described in a company statement as a 'paradigm shift in how effectively PET can be recycled', it is believed the process could revolutionise recycling and is another step towards a 'clean and protected environment for future generations'. The company aims to be using the process to recycle PET on an industrial scale by 2024–25.

The Future Blossoms at Arabic School of New Zealand

A school in Wellington is giving young migrants and refugees the chance to learn Arabic and maintain links with their culture while living in New Zealand. The Arabic School of New Zealand was established to teach Arab children their heritage, language and common values so that they are able to develop a sense of identity, communicate fluently with older relatives and to support bilingualism.

All its students are from families that have moved to New Zealand from Arabic-speaking countries as migrants or refugees and whose parents often do not have time to teach them how to read and write in Arabic.

The school was founded by Mohamed Hilal following his family's own experience of arriving in the country as a refugee. He, his wife Fatima and their two young children escaped the war in Syria, travelling via Malaysia to New Zealand in 2017. Mohamed took English classes with English Language Partners, an organisation providing language lessons and general support to refugees, later going on to study IT at Victoria University. But as they settled into their new life, both realised there was a lack of formal classes for their children to study their native language.

They wanted them to be able to integrate into Kiwi society, but without losing a connection to their culture and language, so in early 2018 they started after-school lessons called Future Blossoms, where children were taught to read and write Arabic. Interest was so great that they soon had to expand their classes across three sites. After overcoming challenges to find teachers, books and premises, the Arabic School of New Zealand was born. The school now has around 200 students aged five to 15 years, taught by volunteers who are native Arabic speakers.

Unlike English, Arabic has many words that are similar but with slightly differing meanings – for example, there are 25 Arabic words for love. As it is also a tonal language, it is best learned from a native speaker as pronunciation can completely change the meaning of a word.

Now parents to a third child, Mohamed and Fatima continue to find more ways to support children and refugee families in education. Mohamed sits on the English Language Partners ethnic advisory group, which informs the national board on migrant and refugee issues, while Fatima is studying English to become a primary school teacher.

First Tribally-associated Medical School Opens in Oklahoma

A college combining the traditional healing practice of the Cherokee people with Western medical training has opened as part of Oklahoma State University. It is the first ever tribally-associated medical school in America and was established after the university heard that funds were being raised for the Cherokee Nation medical system.

Rather than simply investing money in the medical system, the university suggested building a school on a tribal health facility in Tahlequah, which would cater to indigenous American medical students.

The college opened in August 2020 with a mission to 'educate primary care physicians with an emphasis on rural and under-served Oklahoma', welcoming its first intake of 54 first-year students, 20 per cent of whom were American-Indian.

In a statement marking the opening, the Principal Chief of the Cherokee Nation, Chuck Hoskin, Jr., said: 'We know that we will one day look back on this day and what will matter most is whether our efforts have changed lives for the better. I believe that this partnership will advance quality healthcare for all by allowing us to teach a new generation of medical professionals to serve our communities for years to come.'

It is hoped that the school, which will be attended by both indigenous and non-indigenous students, will address the historical inequities and structural failings that negatively impact the health of indigenous Americans and improve their representation in the medical workforce.

Last Danish Circus Elephants Enjoy Retirement

Four former circus elephants purchased by the Danish government have started enjoying their retirement following the country's ban on the use of wild animals in circuses.

Ramboline, Lara, Djunga and Jenny were 'adopted' by the Danish government in 2019, along with a camel named Ali – a long-term friend of Ramboline. The animals were initially looked after by Animal Protection Denmark while a 140,000 square metre (1,506,950 square foot) custom space was prepared for them in Knuthenborg Safaripark on the island of Lolland. Their move to the park marked the end of the exploitation of elephants ahead of the implementation of the ban, which became law in January 2021.

While the four have been getting used to just being elephants, Denmark has continued to make progress on animal rights. As well as advancing its Animal Welfare Bill, in February 2020 it also became the first country in the world to recognise all animals as sentient beings. Following this, the UK introduced a similar bill, which once passed will mean that any new legislation will have to consider the fact that animals can experience feelings such as pain or joy.

The changes in Denmark are in keeping with other efforts to improve animal welfare around the world. The ban on wild animals in circuses has been adopted by 40 countries including Greece, Peru, Mexico, El Salvador, the Netherlands, Costa Rica, Iran and Slovenia.

Farmer Brings Hills Back to Life

An Indonesian farmer who was once called crazy by fellow villagers has succeeded in his mission to bring life back to the local barren hills. Sadiman's mission began 24 years ago, after mountain forest fires and controlled burning to clear land almost dried up the area's rivers and lakes, evaporating vital water resources in the already drought-prone area of Gendol Hill in Central Java.

The lack of rain was so acute that farmers were limited to just one harvest a year. Sadiman wanted to tackle this issue before the area became completely dry. He knew that banyan and ficus trees could store a lot of water, so he began bringing Banyan seeds to his village and bartering the goats he reared for saplings, which he then started planting in the hills.

The long and wide-spreading roots of the trees helped to retain groundwater and stop the land from eroding, but his neighbours still weren't convinced by his plan. Undeterred, Sadiman continued planting, funding his project by growing cloves and jackfruit to sell or barter. Trees started to sprawl across the hills and where the land was once dry, springs began to form.

To date, he has planted 11,000 trees across almost 250 hectares (618 acres) of land. Thanks to Sadiman's single-minded determination, homes in several local villages are now supplied with clean water and local farmers use the water to irrigate their fields. They enjoy two or three harvests each year. Villagers now appreciate Sadiman's work and he holds no grudges about their past opinions. His only hope is that they remain happy and prosperous – and don't burn the forests again.

Canada Launches Nature Prescription Programme

The benefits of spending time in nature have long been extolled, although the idea of a nature prescription is a relatively new one. But in 2021, doctors and other healthcare providers in Canada became able to prescribe time in nature, thanks to the Park Prescriptions or PaRx initiative.

The aim of the initiative is to make prescribing time in nature simple, fun and effective, with its weekly recommended dose of two hours – just 20 minutes per day – significantly improving health and wellbeing. Doctors believe that providing a written prescription, rather than just discussing it during appointments, will make it more likely that people will follow the advice. It is also thought that a prescription for time in nature is more accessible and less overwhelming than traditional exercise prescriptions.

As well as providing resources, tips and patient handouts, the PaRx programme will eventually also allow patients to log their daily outdoor time for doctors to review via an app, providing accountability and a means of motivation.

Canada isn't the first country to try the approach. Nature prescriptions were listed as one of the top global wellness trends in 2019 and in the same year a UK report published by Leeds Beckett University analysing the social value of the Wildlife Trusts' nature conservation projects, found that people participating in outdoor nature conservation activities felt significantly better, both emotionally and physically. The PaRx website warns that side effects of the prescriptions may include: 'living longer, increased energy, reduced stress and anxiety, better mood, pain reduction and improved heart health'.

Father and Son Donate Lungs to Save Mum

A woman has become the first ever COVID-19 patient to receive a living donor lung transplant – from her husband and son.

The world-first procedure took place at Kyoto University Hospital in April 2021 after the previously-healthy woman's lungs failed due to damage caused by the virus. When doctors advised her family that she would need a lung transplant to survive, her husband and son both offered to be living donors, despite the risk of decreased lung capacity.

Lung transplants from donors who had died have been carried out on coronavirus patients in other countries, but because of a lack of donors and long waiting lists in Japan, the woman's family decided to donate part of their lungs to ensure she received treatment in time.

It took 11 hours for surgeons to carry out the surgery. Thankfully, it was a success, with the woman and her donor family members making a full recovery.

Speaking after the operation, the surgeon who led the operation, Doctor Hiroshi Date, highlighted that the procedure had not previously been an option, but now gave hope for others suffering from severe lung damage.

Drug Dramatically Reduces HIV Infection Rate

The use of pre-exposure prophylaxis or PrEP has decreased HIV infections by 70 per cent, according to data compiled by the Global PrEP Network. More than 600,000 people across 76 countries received PrEP at least once in 2019. The drug is taken by people who might be at risk of exposure to HIV, in order to lower their risk of infection.

It works by ensuring that there are high levels of antiretroviral drugs (ARVs) in a person's bloodstream before they are exposed to HIV. Then, if they encounter the virus the drugs prevent it from entering cells and replicating.

Studies into the efficacy of PrEP in England and France, where the drug was taken daily and before and after sex respectively, reduced infections by 86 per cent. PrEP was made available free on the NHS in the UK in October 2020. While there is still a long road ahead in terms of global access to PrEP, this game-changing form of HIV protection is an important step forward in the work towards ending HIV transmissions.

Drones Help to Fight Deforestation

Indigenous people in the Amazon rainforest are fighting deforestation by using drones to identify illegal logging activity.

A team of biologists, foresters, cartographers, anthropologists, journalists and specialists in healthcare and information technology teamed up with WWF International to train Andean tribes living deep within Brazil's rainforest to use the technology. With the help of drones and advisers, the tribespeople can use their ancestral knowledge of the forests to help protect wildlife, identify and collate evidence of illegal logging and use it to file reports on such activities.

Illegal logging has caused many of the wildfires that have devastated rainforests in recent years and the group found a 0.6 hectare (1.4 acre) area of clear-cut land on their first attempt at using the drones.

Continued monitoring later identified a helicopter spreading grass seed, which suggested that the people responsible for clearing the rainforest intended to use the land illegally for cattle grazing.

The WWF and the Kaninde Ethno Environmental Defense Association have run drone operating courses for five indigenous tribes, including the Uru-Eu-Wau-Wau in western Brazil. The project can cost as little as $2,000 for equipment and training per group and allows them to create videos, high-res images and GPS coordinates of logging sites, giving them a fighting chance in the battle against illegal loggers.

The project is yet another small step tipping the balance back towards indigenous tribes fighting against deforestation in the Amazon. In 2020 the Asháninka indigenous people won a lawsuit against illegal logging interests that had rumbled on for almost three decades. The challenges were brought after forestry firms started harvesting mature cedar and mahogany trees in the Kampa do Rio Amônia indigenous Reserve for use in the European furniture trade. The tribe was awarded $3 million in compensation, which will be paid over five years and mainly funnelled into reforestation projects. They were also given a public apology.

Also in 2020, Nemonte Nenquimo, an indigenous Amazon leader, was awarded the Goldman

Environmental Award, known as the Green Nobel Prize. Nemonte led a campaign and legal action that resulted in a court ruling protecting 202,343 hectares (500,000 acres) of Amazonian rainforest and Waorani territory from oil extraction. Her leadership and efforts have set a legal precedent for indigenous rights in Ecuador and her actions have inspired other tribes globally to act against threats to the rainforest.

Welsh Wildlife Haven Thrives After Storm Disaster

As high tides and storms have battered the UK's coastlines, the National Trust, governments and local authorities have been faced with difficult decisions around how to defend, or *not* defend affected areas of around 780 miles of coastline.

When the sea wall enclosing Cwm Ivy Marsh collapsed in August 2014, the latter decision was made and nature was allowed to take its course, with the natural breach in the wall gradually opening and the sea reclaiming the marsh. More than seven years later, the area that was once pasture where sheep grazed is now a thriving salt marsh bursting with flora and fauna.

The decision was not taken lightly, but after public consultation an approach of 'no active intervention' was agreed and the project to recreate almost 40 hectares (100 acres) of new salt marsh habitat and reintegrate it into the wider estuary began. The project was intended to provide important new feeding and resting sites for birds and other wildlife, as well as ensuring that the ecosystems in the nearby Burry Inlet and Carmarthen Bay would be protected long into the future. The approach is now helping to provide 'compensatory habitat' for other salt marsh areas along the coast.

As humans retreated, the tides brought in wildflower seeds and created marshland where otters began to reappear. Rare and threatened species of birds including ospreys, skylarks, lapwings and curlews were spotted and around 150 species of plants began to flourish, helping to tackle climate change by capturing and storing carbon dioxide from the atmosphere.

Cwm Ivy is the only site of its kind in Wales and one of just a few in the UK, but it is part of the National Trust's shifting shores policy, which focuses on working with nature and rather than trying to

simply stop change, plans ahead for it. At present there are 90 hotspots for coastal adaptation across the National Trust's estate, with two or three being actively worked on. As a result of the approach at Cwm Ivy, a significant range of species have now been recorded at the site, with some rare ones even being rediscovered or spotted in new habitats for the first time.

Cleaning Product Vending Machine Leads the 'Refill Revolution'

A Chilean start-up is leading the 'refill revolution' with the launch of cleaning product vending machines that allow customers to ditch single-use plastics and pay only for what they need.

Algramo, which means 'by the gram', buys cleaning products in bulk at a fixed price and dispenses them from vending machines located in stores or mounted on electric tricycles. The company provides reusable bottles with radio frequency identification (RFID) codes, so people can buy as much of the product as they need using the Algramo app and digital wallet, while also receiving a discount for reusing the bottle.

The company is the brainchild of founder José Manuel Moller, who saw the opportunity to provide a cheaper way for low-income families to buy in bulk, while also reducing the amount of packaging waste created by the purchase of smaller-format versions of staple household products. Smaller-format products are often purchased by lower-income households who don't have available funds to buy larger packs, generating more plastic waste. Low-resource areas are also less likely to have good waste management systems in place, meaning that lots of the packaging will end up polluting the environment.

The company has launched pilot schemes in Santiago, New York and Jakarta, and is working with global brands including Unilever and Purina to drive this 'refill revolution'. Unilever reported considerable success during its pilot, with some customers refilling their bottles 15 times – just one Algramo product removing the need for around 2kg (4.4lb) of plastic.

The initiative has been funded by a grant from Closed Loop Ventures, a venture capital firm that invests in start-ups that support its vision for a circular economy – a strategy that ensures all waste products are used in other production systems.

Youth Activists Launch Black Hair Code

A group of 30 young Black activists have challenged hair discrimination by launching the UK's first ever Black hair code. The Halo Code is a pledge that celebrates and protects natural black hair and hairstyles that are connected to Black peoples' racial, ethnic, cultural and religious identities. Employers, professional bodies and schools can sign up to the pledge to be a place that 'champions the right of staff to embrace all Afro-hairstyles' and that will 'celebrate Afro-textured hair worn in all styles' while promising to create a community built on equality and respect 'where hair texture and style have no bearing on an employee's ability to succeed'.

The code was created by the Halo Collective, part of social justice group The Advocacy Academy, which trains young people in activism and politics. The idea came from its founding members' personal experiences of feeling uncomfortable wearing their natural hair at work, being told their hairstyles were 'messy', 'unprofessional' and 'unkempt', and being faced with insensitive questions and comments from their peers.

Despite race-based hair discrimination being illegal in the UK under the Equalities Act 2010, Black people have continued to battle discriminatory workplace and school dress codes and attitudes. However, the Halo Code is making progress towards ending hair discrimination in the UK, with Unilever UK, the Royal Institute of British Architects (RIBA) and a raft of national law firms signing up to the pledge, along with a growing number of schools.

Another young activist campaigning for a change in attitudes towards Black hair is seven-year-old Morgan Bugg from Brentwood, Tennessee. After completing her learning activities on the gamified educational app Freckle, which is used by more than 90,000 teachers across 50 states, she excitedly went to style her personal avatar. But in the virtual store she found no hairstyle options for Black girls like herself and only one for Black boys using the app.

Morgan described feeling 'sad and jealous' that there was no girl hair that reflected her own and decided to vent her frustrations to her teacher.

Understanding her frustration, her teacher asked: 'What can we do to fix it?' and Morgan had an idea. She contacted Freckle and asked them to add Black girl hairstyles to the avatar options, even sending some illustrations as examples. A month later, she received a response: not only was the app going to add hairstyles for Black girls, but they would also use Morgan's illustrations to create them.

Morgan's avatar now proudly has an Afro.

Chernobyl Transformed into Nature Reserve

The area surrounding Chernobyl nuclear plant in Ukraine has been uninhabitable by humans for more than 35 years but in their absence, nature is making a comeback.

Since the worst nuclear accident in human history occurred here, forcing more than 100,000 people from their homes, Chernobyl has been viewed as a place of post-apocalyptic desolation. However, researchers exploring the 2,800 square kilometre (1,081 square mile) Chernobyl Exclusion Zone (CEZ) have found that the area is rewilding and animals including lynx, bison, wolves and deer are thriving.

A six-year project launched in 2015 has helped establish a national biosphere reserve around Chernobyl and worked closely with the Polesskiy Radiation and Ecological Reserve in neighbouring Belarus to create a transboundary protected area. The reserves will allow natural forest to help cleanse contaminated land and waterways in the long term.

Although the Ukrainian government says the area may be unfit for humans for 24,000 years, the resurgence of plantlife in the exclusion zone has provided scientists with a fascinating example of nature's power to bounce back from degradation.

Sergiy Zhyla, Senior Researcher, Chernobyl Biosphere Reserve said: 'Today there is no evidence to suggest that the radioactivity poses any threat to the pH or the other animals here.'

Many endangered animals have been reintroduced to the area to try and help restore the landscape, including the Przewalski's horse, a rare and endangered horse typical of the type that would have roamed the territory 200–300 years ago and similar to the wild horses that lived in the area in prehistoric times.

Thirty horses were introduced in 1998 and now more than 150 live in the exclusion zone. The site is also now the third largest nature reserve in mainland Europe. It is hoped that continuing research and projects on the site will help to develop policies to reverse environmental degradation and prevent future man-made disasters, while also encouraging other countries to sustainably manage forests, combat desertification, reverse land degradation and halt biodiversity loss.

'Mindwriting' Now Possible for Paralysed People

Scientists at Stanford University, California, have combined cutting-edge technology and human mental effort to allow a man with full-body paralysis to 'write' with his mind – a technique that has been dubbed 'mindwriting'.

The scientists took artificial intelligence (AI) software and coupled it with two 'brain-computer interface' (BCI) chips – each containing 100 electrodes. These chips were then implanted in the left side of the man's brain and he was asked to imagine writing individual letters of the alphabet on a notepad, with a pen. As he repeated each letter ten times, allowing the AI software to 'learn' the signals associated with each one, the electrodes were able to pick up instructions from neurons firing in the part of the motor cortex that governs hand movement. Algorithms were then used to transcribe the man's thoughts into text on a computer screen.

In later sessions, the man was instructed to copy sentences that the algorithms had not been exposed to; he was asked to provide answers to open-ended questions that required some thought before responding and was presented with groups of sentences and instructed to make a mental effort to 'write' them out. The technology eventually allowed him to generate text at a rate of 18 words per minute. In comparison, able-bodied people of the same age can use smartphones to text at a rate of 23 words per minute.

The study, published in the journal *Nature* in May 2021, shows significant progress in the field. Lead author Frank Willett said: 'We've learned that the brain retains its ability to prescribe fine movements a full decade after the body has lost its ability to execute those movements.'

While not yet available for commercial use, the technology offers hope for those who have lost the use of their upper limbs or the ability to speak due to spinal cord injuries, strokes or other conditions and could spur on future advances.

Shelter Connects Disabled Children and Animals

After Jamie Wallace-Griner's autistic six-year-old son Jackson was given an Autism Service Dog called Angel, she was inspired to set up an animal shelter with a difference. Like many other animal shelters, Safe in Austin rescues neglected and abused animals and helps to rehabilitate them, rehoming those who can be rehomed and providing a safe and loving forever home for those who cannot. But amazed by the positive changes Angel inspired in her son, Jamie decided to use the shelter to connect Safe in Austin's furred and feathered residents with children with similar need.

Speaking of the shelter, Jamie says: 'We invite hearts that need some healing to come and meet the animals, hear their stories, hug their necks, pet their bellies and find connection in a relationship that is without judgement or fear.'

The shelter is located on a ranch in the Texan city of Leander and is home to almost 160 disabled animals, including a potbelly pig called Peter, a lamb and a cow in wheelchairs, a rabbit, a one-legged dog called Halo and a dog called Duchess, who was rescued from a dog-fighting ring and now happily plays mum to puppies, kittens, ducklings, chicks, bunnies and even the shelter's resident tortoise.

Speaking about Safe in Austin's approach, Jamie said: 'Our rescues are grateful and happy and they all have a story to tell. Kids and young adults that come from trauma can relate to the past of these animals and find hope in the future for both of them. At-risk youth see an example of forgiveness and connection they have never felt before and slowly their hearts start to soften. Special needs children find comfort and encouragement when learning about the special needs of many of our animals and learning how we all belong to each other no matter our differences.'

For the first four years of the shelter's life, Jamie and her family paid for the care of the animals. But very recently the organisation has become a non-profit, allowing it to accept donations so that it can rescue more animals and transform the lives of even more vulnerable children and young people.

Photographer Puts Zimbabwe on the (Google) Map

When photographer and film-maker Tawanda Kanhema tried to show a friend his childhood home in Harare, Zimbabwe, he discovered it was not visible on Google Maps Street View. Rather than simply moving on from the disappointment, Tawanda realised that it was something many other people might experience and so he wanted to do something about it. He contacted Google and told them not just about Zimbabwe's absence, but also 14 other countries in the southern Africa region.

In 2018, Tawanda learned about Google's camera loan scheme, which allows people to borrow a camera to capture interesting places, and decided to take one back home to Zimbabwe.

Holding the camera out of the window of his brother's car as they drove around the city, Tawanda managed to collect around 30 miles worth of footage as a pilot shoot to show the potential of his idea. On his return, he undertook six months of training in San Francisco before returning to Zimbabwe for two weeks, where he collected another 2,000 miles of highways and attractions.

This time Tawanda filmed alone, followed by a

Google team who watched how he filmed more challenging locations, for example, flying over Victoria Falls in a helicopter to capture 360-degree footage, using a speedboat to map the Zambezi River and cycling across the Victoria Falls Bridge.

Tawanda believes that as well as being important for navigation purposes, maps today also have an important role in helping people to connect and tell stories and even the smallest contribution can have a significant impact. Speaking to *Good Morning America*, he said: 'The most compelling thing for me is hearing from people who are using these images to help them share a memory from their lives. I hear from people who say: "I was able to show my daughter the home in which I grew up" or "I was able to show my kids the hospital in which I was born." Just being able to hear that people are using maps not just for navigation and finding places, they're using maps to make a connection.'

Tawanda is now responsible for 500 miles of Street View maps available across Zimbabwe, but he refused to stop after mapping his home country. He continues to improve the representation of places around the world through his work and has helped to map Namibia and Northern Ontario.

Australian Earthship Brings Off-the-grid Living to Town

Is it a bird, is it a plane? No, despite the fact its name conjures up images of a terrestrial home for alien lifeforms, 'earthships' are in fact the ultimate in sustainable living and one is making waves in the Australian town of Goolwa.

Earthships are powered by renewable sources like solar panels, wind turbines and biodiesel generators, while also using the climate, sun and local terrain to generate natural heat and cooling. They often collect their own drinking water, treat their own sewage and even grow their own food. Most are found in remote off-the-grid areas. High school teacher Amy Mackenzie wanted her home to be completely self-sustainable, yet still just a short walk to the shops or work, so that she could maintain a connection to her community. After finding a suitable plot of land in a residential area of Goolwa, she began constructing her own earthship in 2020, using tyres, cans, glass bottles and other recycled materials.

Amy first became interested in sustainable construction after coordinating a volunteer programme in Nicaragua, where plastic bottles were used to build a school, creating an eco-friendly building that also provided a sense of shared ownership among those who helped to build it. She later attended the Earthship Academy in New Mexico, USA, where she learned more about the buildings from the American architect Michael Reynolds.

Amy's home, which will be the first of its kind in a residential area of South Australia, will use repurposed car tyres in the same way as bricks and there will also be straw-bale walls on the east and west side of the house and a stained-glass window created using glass bottles. Local residents have shown keen interest in Amy's project, coming to view the plans she has placed outside the site, attending open nights about the earthship and volunteering their skills at various stages of the build.

Speaking to local newspaper, the *Victor Harbor Times*, Amy said: 'The great thing about earthships is that they are a community build and it's not just about the home itself, but the community of people who come and help.'

As well as reducing pressure on non-renewable building resources and benefitting from the use of only eco-friendly means of generating electricity, earthships are largely customisable, so owners can tailor the design to their unique needs, from how the building looks to the number of plants they wish to grow.

When Amy's earthship is complete it will become one of around 3,000 fully-built earthships existing in the world today.

Company Puts Best Foot Forward with Sock Recycling Scheme

An eco-conscious company has come up with an ingenious use for one of the most frequently wasted textiles – old socks! A survey conducted by Colorado-based Smartwool revealed that while more than 80 per cent of respondents recycled used clothing, 91 per cent were throwing away one or more pairs of socks each year, contributing to the enormous amount of textile waste that ends up in landfill.

Understanding that socks see significant wear and tear and are often unfit for donation, and that most people wouldn't want to wear second-hand socks, the US company eyed a different audience and identified a way to transform old socks into cosy dog beds.

It set up a scheme where people could drop off used socks, of any brand and in any condition, at donation banks, or post them direct to Smartwool. The old socks were then deconstructed by a process which grinds down waste fibres before putting them through a machine to create yarn which can then be knitted or woven, or turned into filling, insulation or acoustic material. The donated socks were recycled into the latter, with the resultant filling being used to stuff snug dog beds for pampered pets.

Company bosses described the scheme as 'just the beginning' and the first of many that will come from Smartwool's new initiative, the Second Cut Project. The initiative is intended to give waste textiles a second life and keep good materials out of landfill, with the ultimate aim of making all of its products circular by 2030.

Coral Replanting Breathes Life into Belize Reef

When marine biologist Lisa Carne founded non-profit organisation Fragments of Hope, she wanted nothing more than to help restore coral reefs through replanting. She established the company in 2013 but her mission had started many years earlier, after learning how Hurricane Iris had destroyed large swathes of coral reef off the coast of Belize in 2001. Lisa had been lucky enough to experience their beauty and importance to local eco-systems prior to the storm and began single-handedly planting corals, with the aim of bringing the reef back to life.

She began to push for large-scale replanting initiatives, but it took several years until she was able to secure the funding required. Lisa then formed a team that started to take viable pieces of coral and grow them into transplant segments. As the corals started to spawn, local fishermen and tour guides from nearby Placencia village began to sit up and take notice and volunteer their time to help.

Eighty per cent of the corals from that first initiative continue to thrive today, having survived tropical storms and a Category 1 hurricane. A total of 85,000 corals have been planted in the area to date, increasing the coral cover from 6 to 50 per cent between 2010 and 2017.

The techniques advocated by Fragments of Hope and used in Belize have now also been used to restore reefs in areas of Colombia, Jamaica and the Caribbean island of St Barts. The replanting efforts in Belize have now also been supported by legal protections for the

coral reefs, including bans on shrimp trawling, the use of gill nets and off-shore oil exploration.

Wales Appoints World's First Non-Binary Mayor

The city of Bangor in North Wales made history in 2021 when it elected a non-binary candidate to be mayor, presiding over a population of more than 16,000 people.

Twenty-three-year-old Owen J. Hurcum is agender, genderqueer and non-binary, with the latter being an umbrella term for gender identities that are outside the gender binary – so neither male nor female. Their election comes just two years after coming out and following the announcement they expressed their pride in the city's decision.

In a post on Twitter, accompanied by a photo of them wearing their chains of office, a sheer black shirt and colourful green hair poking from beneath a tricorne hat, Owen said: 'When I came out two years ago, I was so worried I'd be ostracised by my community or worse. Today my community elected me

Mayor of our great City. The youngest ever Mayor in Wales. The first ever openly non-binary Mayor of any city anywhere.'

A day later, they continued: 'I know representation is not just putting on the chain and I'll be judged by what we do as a team for Bangor during my year in office, but still, glad my election has resonated with so many.'

Prior to their election, Owen had been active in politics and their community for five years, as a councillor in the city for four years before being appointed deputy mayor in 2020. Although there is still much work to be done in terms of representation of diverse genders and the LGBTQ+ community around the world, progress is being made, bringing hope to many.

In May 2021, Deputy Press Secretary Karine Jean-Pierre became the first gay woman – and the second ever Black woman – to lead a White House press briefing, while in April of that year, two transgender candidates, M. Radha and Bharathi Kannamma, both contested in Assembly polls in Tamil Nadu, a state in southern India. In Brazil, an ordained pastor, Jacque Chanel, founded the country's first ever transgender church.

Change is also apparent in popular culture, with

Germany's *Next Top Model* crowning its first-ever transgender winner, 23-year-old Alex-Mariah Peter from Cologne, and a Paramount+ reboot of iconic Nickelodeon cartoon *Rugrats* brought back popular character Betty – mum to naughty twin toddlers Phil and Lil – as an out-and-proud lesbian.

Australian Brings Ancient Tree Back from the Brink of Extinction

While studying aromatic medicine, Tuesday Browell discovered an interesting line in one of her books, indicating that a northern sandalwood tree could be found in her hometown of Torrumbarry, Australia, on an old sandhill.

For centuries exploited for their aromatic wood and oil, the trees were at the brink of extinction in the state of Northern Victoria, so Tuesday decided to trek to the location to find out if this particular tree was still alive and well. Arriving at the sandhill, she found the rare and endangered tree flourishing – along with 14 others.

Tuesday bought the land and placed a conservation covenant on it, to ensure that the trees could never be removed, before starting to tend the soil around the ancient trees. In time, more new saplings popped up and now almost 50 sandalwood trees grow on the property. The sandalwood tree is tricky to propagate as it is a little like a parasite and needs a host tree to grow in. If that tree dies, it needs to find another, or it will die too.

Despite these difficulties, the trees continue to thrive and provide a boost for the species, whose numbers had dropped to just one per cent of the sandalwood trees that once grew in Northern Victoria. Although unassuming in appearance, they were prized for their expensive wood and oil, and in the 1800s large numbers were felled and exported to China and other parts of Asia. Following her find, Tuesday also called for more protection for the trees from the state government. Fences and pest control measures were introduced and support provided to help more trees to grow.

Tuesday's find isn't the only good plant news to come out of Australia in 2021. Critically endangered pot-bellied greenhood orchids, which only flower for a couple of weeks a year or sometimes not at all, have been found in the New South Wales Southern

Highlands. The cluster of about 170 orchids is believed to have thrived due to the wet summer and is now being monitored and preserved by specialists in threatened species.

Master Falconer Rehabilitates Young People at Risk

By his own admission, Rodney Stotts doesn't look like the falconer and conservationist type, but it's a passion that has transformed his life. Now, he's using his skills to help at-risk children.

Born in Washington, USA, as a young man Rodney started along the only path he knew – drug dealing. It was a route he might have continued on, until – after having to attend 33 funerals in one year – he realised his lifestyle was not safe nor sustainable.

As he moved away from his old life, he rented an apartment and needed to find a job to secure his home. Fate led him to work for a non-profit organisation called Earth Conservation Corps, which was dedicated to cleaning up pollution in the Anacostia River and conserving local wildlife, which in turn introduced him to working with falcons and other birds of prey. It was here that Rodney's passion blossomed and he began rehabilitating injured birds of prey.

Speaking to *Voice of America News*, he said: 'I think that's what I was given. I was that bird that had to go through rehabilitation. And once I was rehabilitated, I was released back into the wild with more knowledge now than before.'

After gaining his falconry licence, Rodney was put in charge of the birds of prey programme at Earth Conservation Corps and started working with youth rehabilitation centres and programmes supporting at-risk children and young people.

In regular sessions, children facing substance abuse and issues with violence are invited to the Earth Conservation Corps campus to feed birds and see Rodney training, handling and caring for the birds of prey. The sessions are also an opportunity for him to share his stories, provide hope and help these youngsters connect their lives and paths to those of Rodney's birds, to help them believe that they too are capable of change.

Rodney, who now also runs his own non-profit called Rodney's Raptors, continues to work as a licensed falconer, mentor and youth community leader, creating opportunities to connect young people to the environment and their community, and helping to break harmful cycles.

Speaking in *The Falconer*, a PBS documentary about his life, he highlighted the importance of falconry in his life and the lives of others, saying: 'That connection though. I'm taking care of something. There's a love that comes with it. You start to feel appreciated and, you know, that can turn you around indefinitely.'

Japanese Museum Plays Host to Feline Stand-off

In a world so often filled with conflict and opposition, one Japanese museum is playing host to what may be the most adorable stand-off in history. Since 2017, Sadao Umayahara, a security guard at the Onomichi City Museum of Art in Hiroshima, has had to refuse entry to two very persistent would-be patrons – a tabby cat called Go-chan and a black tomcat called Ken-chan.

Ken-chan first tried to break into the museum in 2017, when its Catful Exhibit was showing. He returned with Go-chan in tow for later attempts to sneak past security and the epic – but tender – battle between man and beast went viral.

Exactly why these two feline friends are so keen to gain entry is unknown, although the museum's curator has speculated that the photographs of black cats that were displayed in the museum's windows – or the venue's air-conditioning – may have piqued their interest. Now the cats, which usually only appear when Sadao is on duty, are a regular feature outside the museum and are considered by some as unofficial mascots.

Since their first visit, Sadao has had to enforce the museum's strict no-animals policy, gently blocking their wily attempts to sneak past him, picking them off entrance mats and always offering some tickles to soften the blow.

Sadao's gentle attempts to discourage the cats seem to have created an affectionate bond – and a little bit of jealousy – between the two cats. In one video shared on Twitter, where Ken-chan and Go-chan appear to be vying for his attention, Sadao crouches down to mediate, saying, 'You have to get along' as he pets them.

Following the lifting of coronavirus lockdown restrictions in 2020, after a two-month hiatus – the stand-off resumed and once again went viral. The security guard's approach to conflict resolution has captured the attention and hearts of people around the world. Lots of the museum's 45,000 Twitter followers are pushing for it to grant the cats admission, but many just want everyone to be a bit more like Sadao Umayahara.

Manmade Island Allows Escape from the City

A manmade island constructed on a pier in Manhattan, New York, is allowing people to escape the city without ever leaving it. Designer Thomas Heatherwick and his team were initially invited to design a pavilion for the traditional flat pier, previously known as Pier 55. Instead, working with the project's private funders, he came up with a very different idea for the public space.

That idea was Little Island – a park built over the Hudson River that aimed to create an immersive experience with nature and art, whisking people away from the hustle and bustle of the city and giving them 'the feeling of actually leaving Manhattan behind'.

Only accessible by gangplank bridges, the three-dimensional construction incorporates an undulating landscape that is alpine-like at its highest point of 19 metres (62 feet), but also features more protected and shaded areas, with all areas populated with hundreds of varieties of flowers and plants. The island is supported by 132 concrete piles built up from the river between the leftover wood piles of Pier 54 and Pier 56, which were preserved to maintain the habitats of local wildlife.

Little Island, which opened to the public in June 2021, is now home to two performance areas, including an amphitheatre. Its first ever programme included theatre, music and dance performances and creative workshops for children and adults.

Access to the island is free, while a fee is charged to watch performances, with subsidised tickets available to residents from Harlem, the Bronx and neighbouring boroughs, to ensure that the island and its programme is accessible to all.

The project – which was almost a decade in the making – was largely privately funded by businessman Barry Diller and his wife, designer Diane Von Furstenberg, through their foundation. The foundation has also committed to pay for the maintenance of the structure for the next 20 years.

Speaking of his initial vision, Barry said: 'What was in my mind was to build something for the people of New York and for anyone who visits – a space that on first sight was dazzling and upon use made people happy.'

Designer Thomas Heatherwick has spoken openly about the lack of public spaces being commissioned by governments and local authorities, saying that they have 'lost their confidence' to create new, innovative public spaces, leaving much in the hands of private investors. While sometimes controversial, he argues that privately-funded projects like Little Island allow architects and designers to advocate for public amenities and provide variety. The hope is that this project inspires many more public spaces like it.

Dutch Bee Stops Tackle Declining Population

In the Dutch city of Utrecht hundreds of local bus stops are topped with a roof filled with beautiful wildflowers – but their purpose isn't aesthetic. The 316 flower-topped bus stops are actually bee sanctuaries, aimed at tackling the country's declining bee population. Dubbed 'bee stops', the otherwise ordinary bus shelters are planted with grass and wildflowers to encourage pollination, capture fine dust and store rainwater and attract honeybees and bumblebees that can support the city's biodiversity. The bee stops require little maintenance, but when they need it, they are tended to by workers who drive around the city in electric vehicles.

The Netherlands is home to 358 different species of bee, yet more than half of them are endangered and the bee stop scheme is just one of Utrecht's initiatives to support their survival. Residents can also apply for funding to create similar bee sanctuaries on their own roofs.

Bee-friendly bus stops are also appearing in the UK. In 2021, Leicester City Council introduced 12 bus stops with 'living roofs' planted with a mix of wildflowers and sedum plants, making it the first city in the nation to commit to such a scheme.

TikTok Star with Bionic Arm Normalises Limb Difference

For many years, Laiken Olive tried to hide the fact that they were disabled. Born without part of their right arm and often subjected to bullying, the non-binary South Louisianan opted for a cosmetic prosthetic arm covered by jackets to try and hide their disability. But after receiving a state-of-the-art bionic arm inspired by Venom Snake – a character from the video game Metal Gear Solid – Laiken is now working to normalise limb difference by proudly showing off their 'Hero Arm', created by British company Open Bionics. Unlike Venom Snake's iconic black and red arm, Laiken's does not come with weapons, but it has given them the superpower of confidence – a gift they are determined to share.

After realising their personal potential but noticing that they didn't often see people like themselves represented, they set up a TikTok account under the name @thebionicbabe. They started posting videos of themselves cosplaying as Venom Snake and using their bionic arm in everyday situations, from lifting weights to playing with their son. They also shared videos without their prosthetic, instead wearing creative alternatives, including 'sword arm', a 'cottagecore' arm made of flowers and branches, and an ornate 'mushroom fairy arm'.

In one inspirational video captioned 'watch me grow into owning my disability rather than hiding it', and set over a sound track stating how wasted potential 'crushes your spirit', Laiken posted a series of photos of them from childhood to the present day, with their arm hidden in earlier photos, but proudly displayed in later ones.

Within a year they had attracted an audience of more than 29,000 followers and received more than a million views. Laiken now uses their platform to engage with others with limb difference, answering questions from people who want to learn more and speaking out against ableism in everyday life and also the movie industry, where able-bodied actors are often cast in disabled roles.

Despite receiving some negative comments on their platform, Laiken remains unphased, telling the *Washington Post*: 'They're still seeing me. They still know I exist and people like me exist. In the end, that was all I really want.'

Laiken continues to aim to normalise limb-difference though their videos, art, creative sculptures of arms and writing a screenplay about 'finding the limb-different community'.

Fanfare for Trumpeter Swan Back from the Brink

A dedicated group of volunteers working together for more than 40 years have brought a rare swan back from the brink of extinction. The trumpeter swan, North America's largest waterfowl, was almost extinct in Canada until the team at Trumpeter Swan Restoration Group began work to protect and propagate the species.

Numbers began to dwindle in the 1800s, with the last wild trumpeter swan in Ontario being recorded as shot in 1886. It was in 1982 that the species' journey back from the brink began, when retired biologist Harry Lumsden received a shipment of trumpeter eggs.

A founding member of the Ontario-based restoration group, Harry and dozens of volunteers used the eggs to launch a captive breeding programme on the Wye Marsh. Once the eggs hatched, the cygnets needed to be raised and closely monitored. The volunteers tracked and raised the birds, following their family trees – and love lives – with interest.

With its enormous wingspan, which can reach up to eight feet across, and distinctive party horn honk, the bird was easily recognisable, but the breeding programme faced challenges, so the volunteers worked to mitigate risks to the birds, such as lead poisoning, power lines, hunting and poaching.

In winter 2021, after almost four decades of dedication, around 1,200 swans returned to Ontario for their mating season. While still a fragile species, the signs for the future are hopeful. The group continues to protect, monitor and advocate for the birds, which is also seeing a resurgence in numbers in parts of the United States.

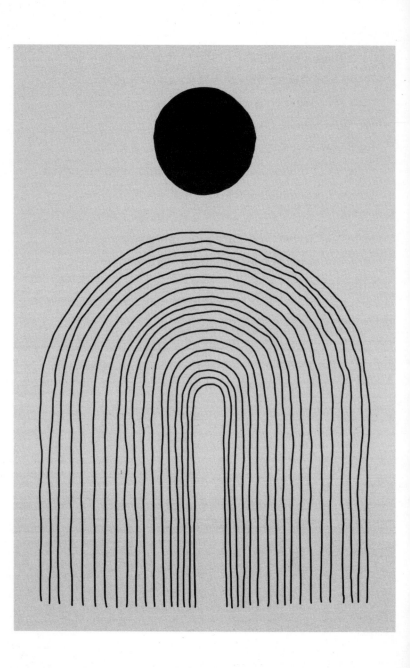

New Marine Parks to Protect Ocean Area Bigger Than 91 Million Football Pitches

Two new marine parks in Australia will protect 740,736 square metres (286,000 square miles) of ocean. Australia's marine parks are protected areas located within the country's waters and managed by its government. The new parks will be established around Christmas Island and the Cocos (Keeling) Islands in the Indian Ocean. Both islands are recognised globally as natural wonders, with Christmas Island famed for its red crab migration.

The establishment of the protected areas will provide vital protection for diverse marine life and support the two islands' local communities, which rely on sustainable fishing to maintain their livelihoods and way of life. It will also support and promote eco-tourism, further benefitting local businesses and fishers. The Australian government has allocated $5.4 million in grants to promote and manage the marine parks after their establishment – for ranger positions, community engagement and marine and research projects.

The creation of the two new marine parks will mean that the percentage of waters under protection will increase from 37 to 45 per cent, making Australia a global leader in ocean protection.

Trafficked Turtles Returned Home Using DNA Tests

Distinctive, valuable turtles trafficked illegally around the globe are being returned to their natural habitat using rapid DNA tests.

South American Matamata freshwater turtles are prized for their unusual appearance – a rough, knobbly shell and ridged neck – and often sold illegally for significant sums in Europe, Asia, and the US. Colombian officials are tasked with stopping the turtles being trafficked, but if they are returned to the wrong river basin, they can damage the delicate natural ecosystem and native turtle populations. Although they are easy to spot, identifying which specific basin the striking creatures come from is a more challenging task.

To solve this problem, marine scientist Demian Chapman developed a low-cost DNA test that can take a simple swab and identify the origin of turtles in just two hours. For just one dollar per sample, researchers can then identify where the turtles came from and get them back to their natural habitat.

The tests, which researchers eventually hope to make more widely available around the world, have helped to identify and return 2,000 Matamata turtles to their Orinoco River basin home. They are also used to reveal the origin of illegally traded shark meat and trafficked European eels.

Volunteers Turn Plastic Waste into Library for Orphans

Plastic waste donated locally from a neighbourhood in Myanmar, South East Asia, has been transformed into a stunning library for orphaned children. A team of volunteers from the NGO Clean Yangon used the rubbish to create 5,000 eco-bricks – plastic bottles stuffed with more shredded plastic waste, such as plastic bags and other packaging.

Each eco-brick took approximately one hour to make, with some completing hundreds during the project. The volunteers marked each one they completed with their name, before it was installed in the structure, proudly highlighting their contribution and becoming part of the fabric of the building. The eventual beneficiaries of the project, local orphans from the neighbourhood of Taikkyi, were able to watch as the project progressed and learn the innovative and sustainable technique to create building materials.

The building was completed in May 2021. The volunteers expressed hope that the structure would soon be filled with books and ready for the children to use. They also hoped that their efforts would encourage the youngsters to think creatively to find eco-friendly solutions to save the planet. Other charities are taking a similar approach to plastic waste in Myanmar, with the Badana Aid Foundation using the same process to build a school in Hlaingthaya Township in Yangon.

Friends Make One Per Cent Go a Long, Long Way

An idea that started between friends in the UK in 2011 has raised more than half a million pounds to help people in need all around the world. Concerned about the issue of global poverty, Liverpool residents Matt Johnson and Steve Pilgrim asked a few of their friends to donate just one per cent of their income each month, so they could see how many people they could help with the collective contribution.

Between eight people, they raised £166. While this might seem like a nominal amount, Matt and Steve discovered that it was enough to pay for malaria treatments for 332 people. From this, Be One Percent was born. The pair formally established the charity, asked more people to start donating and gathered a board of trustees who would be responsible for allocating grants to charities providing life-changing and life-saving initiatives.

The criteria they created were clear: their charity partners needed to be efficient in tackling different poverty issues in the developing world. They also needed to be either delivering specific resources on the ground or have a high charitable spend to ensure that member donations' would be used as effectively as possible.

Designed to be accessible to people of all incomes, the charity operates on a shoestring, with overheads covered by business partners and operations run mainly by volunteers, so that 100 per cent of member donations go to the people and projects that need it.

Each year the organisation creates a calendar of 12 projects that address diverse global issues, including malaria, food poverty, access to water and slavery. Since its inception in 2011, it has worked with anti-slavery charity Hope for Justice, Against Malaria, Deki, an ethical micro-loan provider working at grassroots level and OneDollarGlasses.

Now celebrating its tenth year, Be One Percent has 202 members. It has raised £634,000, funded 124 projects and reached more than half a million people – not bad for an idea born between friends!

Silent Bakery Challenges Disability Stereotypes

A silent bakery in the Chinese city of Wuhan, capital of Central China's Hubei province, is bringing people together to share skills and tackle negative stereotypes about disabled people.

Pica Pica, which means magpie in Chinese, focuses on employing people with hearing impairments who have excellent communication and writing skills and a knowledge of the baking industry. The business was established by Tan Ting after meeting a group of students with physical and learning disabilities at a charity baking course. Tan was inspired by their upbeat attitude and the attention they paid to the course, but also aware of negative stereotypes portraying disabled people as disadvantaged and a social burden.

She began researching job opportunities and education for hearing impaired people, visiting silent workplaces that had opened in other major Chinese cities and undertaking the necessary training to allow her to open her own. As well as baking and serving fresh produce to customers, Tan's team also go into local communities, nursing homes and schools to provide free baking courses, organising about five events each month.

Getting a job at Pica Pica isn't easy though. As a commercial business and not a charity, Tan searches hard to find the very best staff. Twenty-seven-year-old cashier Wan Xiaohui, who lost her hearing at birth, faced a three-hour written test and in-person interview before becoming part of the team. Tan reveals that the name of the bakery is a nod to her employee base. Magpies represent a tough-minded personality and are symbols of joy and good luck in Chinese culture. She said: 'Hearing-impaired employees cannot engage with the world through sound, but they always embrace the world with smiles.'

Pica Pica is one of a growing number of businesses focused on hiring people with disabilities, with more opening up in Beijing, Shanghai, Guangzhou and Changsha. This shift is not only providing more career options for disabled people and helping them to realise their own value, but also challenging negative stereotypes that have held them back for too long.

To date, Tan's silent bakery has employed eight hearing-impaired staff members and some have gone on to launch their own businesses in the industry.

Blind People Improve Navigation Skills by Mimicking Dolphins

Researchers are exploring how blind people could improve their ability to navigate, by using the same techniques as dolphins. Echolocation is the technique that creatures such as dolphins, whales and bats use to emit sounds that bounce off objects and come back, giving them vital information about what's around them. Researchers at Durham University in England have been exploring the technique and how it could be used to give blind and visually-impaired people greater independence.

While it is already proven that humans can use the technique – expert echolocators already exist – the study focused specifically on how easy the technique is for humans to learn and whether that learning is affected by the age of the subject.

Over a ten-week period, 12 blind and 14 sighted volunteers aged between 21 and 79 were taught the technique of making clicking sounds using their mouth, walking stick or footsteps. The training also involved teaching the participants how to distinguish the size of objects, orientation perception and virtual navigation. The study found that all participants were able to improve their ability to navigate using the technique, with some achieving comparable levels of competency with echolocators who had been using the techniques for a decade. Neither age nor visual impairment was found to be an obstruction to learning echolocation.

A post-study survey found an enthusiastic response to the approach, with 87 per cent of participants saying that their independence and wellbeing had improved significantly, while all of the blind participants stated that their mobility had improved.

The results have been welcomed by researchers, who believe that the confidence of participants to use the technique in social situations means there is less stigma associated with it than they had believed. It is now hoped that click-based echolocation training could provide a valuable skill for those with degenerative sight conditions, allowing them to learn the technique while they still have some functional vision.

New Artificial Palm Oil Could Help Save Forests

A man-made version of the palm oil found in many of our everyday foods and products could prevent deforestation. Palm oil is used in everything from biscuits and chocolates to shampoo and make-up. Over the last 30 years, half of its plantation growth – much of it in Indonesia – has come at the expense of rainforests, peatland and the indigenous communities and diverse, rare animal species that live there.

Now one biotech company has developed a potential solution – a synthetic alternative as versatile as natural palm oil that doesn't require forests to be destroyed for its production. C16 Biosciences has taken food waste and industrial by-products and used genetically-engineered microbes to convert them into a product that is chemically similar to natural palm oil.

Scientists at the company explain that microbes are a yeast, which they feed with sugars so they grow and produce large quantities of oil within their cells, which can then be extracted. Currently, synthetic palm oil is two to three times more expensive than the natural version, but C16 Biosciences believe that their solution combined with their technology platform could make this version scalable and more competitive in terms of cost.

Not all companies which produce natural palm oil are linked to the destruction of tropical forests and peatland. Some have adopted policies that promise no deforestation, no peat and no exploitation (NDPE) and produce sustainable or 'clean' palm oil. Those who are linked to deforestation produce what is widely known as 'dirty' palm oil.

The World Wildlife Fund (WWF) estimates that the global consumption of palm oil will rise to between 264 and 447 million tonnes by 2050, so a cost-competitive, synthetic alternative – combined with environmental campaigns to stop the production of 'dirty' palm oil – could be a vital tool in the fight to prevent the destruction of our precious and biodiverse rainforests.

Masters Students Strive for 'Peequality' with Women's Urinal

When festival-loving students Amber Probyn and Hazel McShane were asked to solve a real-life problem as part of their masters' project, they had the perfect idea. After spending many summers working at music festivals in the UK, the pair often had to choose between going to the loo or getting food on their breaks, due to 'insane' queues for the women's toilets.

While studying at the University of Bristol, their research revealed that women spent 30 times longer than men waiting to use toilet facilities and they set about creating a solution that would bring about 'pee equality' so women would no longer face long queues for the toilet at festivals, sports events, theatres and in parks.

The pair spoke to more than 2,000 women in focus groups and pubs around Bristol before creating the

'Peequal' – the first ever women's urinal, described as being 'designed for women and co-created by women'. Unlike previous attempts at resolving this age-old problem, often involving funnels and open-air peeing, Amber and Hazel took the concept of a squat toilet and created what they call 'the pedestal'.

Designed like a boat 'to minimise splash back' and featuring a place to hold clothing at the front, the pedestal is housed in waist-height, semi-private, open structures called wedges to offer privacy as well as quick passage and visibility for safety reasons. Its creators claim that it is six times quicker to use than a standard lockable toilet and it boasts few touch points, making it more sanitary.

Peequal units are also made locally from recycled material and are 100 per cent recyclable at the end of an eight-year lifecycle. They can be easily flat-packed for transportation and create 98 per cent less CO_2 than portable toilets.

The prototype was trialled at Bristol Comedy Garden in 2021 and has already gained support from influential organisations and events, including Glastonbury. While Amber and Hazel admit the design might not be for everyone at first, they are convinced people will think differently 'after a few bevs' and when they realise how efficient the Peequal is.

The pair continue to develop the design and strive for 'peequality' for women everywhere.

Popcorn Offers Eco-friendly Packaging Solution

A researcher from Germany found an unlikely replacement for environmentally-damaging plastic packaging while enjoying a snack at a cinema.

As Alireza Kharazipour tucked into the popcorn he had bought to enjoy with a movie, he noticed how the food's structure was similar to commonly-used polystyrene packing peanuts. The next day, he made some popcorn at home and pondered the thought further, before taking the idea into laboratories at the University of Göttingen, where he was a professor in the Faculty of Forest Sciences and Forest Ecology.

Using crushed corn sourced from the inedible by-products of cornflake production, the team used a steam process to expand it into what they called granulated popcorn. From there, they used different moulds to shape the popcorn and coated it in a layer of bioplastic so that it would be water repellent.

Both polystyrene and the popcorn substitute are mainly made of air. But, as the former is manufactured using petroleum, it is difficult to recycle and can take thousands of years to decompose, leaving behind microplastics that are harmful to wildlife. The popcorn packaging, on the other hand, can be reused, shredded or even composted at home. It is hoped that the sustainable packaging, which can be made from by-products or corn that is grown anywhere, could replace vast quantities of packaging and even be used to make take-away food containers. The team is now in discussions to use the material commercially, so it could 'pop' up in a parcel or takeaway near you very soon.

Dutch 'Pig Whisperer' Aims to End Factory Farming

When pigs at 61-year-old Kees Scheepens' farm urinate in their designated pee toilet, they are instantly rewarded with sour lemon candies.

Encouraging the pigs to do their 'number one' and 'number two' businesses in separate places is more than just a hygiene issue, it's helping the environment. When the two are combined, nitrogen produced from the resulting ammonia is partly deposited, causing a loss of biodiversity, something the Dutch government is taking action to prevent.

Kees considers everything at his farm in Oirschot in the southern Netherlands, not least the wellbeing of the pigs he breeds. The 19th generation of farmers in his family and a former vet, Kees does not farm for financial gain, but is instead motivated by 'emancipating farm animals'. He started his pig farm ten years ago with the aim of creating a sustainable and humane alternative to factory farming, where tightly-packed pigs begin to display cannibalistic tendencies such a tail biting, replacing normal pig behaviour.

Kees advocates a natural environment, where pigs can wallow, laze and root around in straw and woodchips in the open air. His turning point came after being forced to euthanise around 10,000 healthy newborn piglets during the swine flu epidemic of 1997–98. The action conflicted with his principles as a trained vet – committed to saving, not slaughtering animals.

Kees believes that the cruelty of factory farms and abattoirs cannot last. Animal welfare and sustainability are now at the heart of his pig farm – home to 28 sows, including seven-year-old Oma or granny – and his affection for the animals has earned him the nickname 'pig whisperer'.

He believes that while finances are a driving factor for many farmers, they should also consider making changes that will maintain proud farming traditions, end factory farming and help save the earth.

Life-saving Rat Retires from Landmine Detection

A specially trained rat that has spent an illustrious career sniffing out landmines and saving lives has gone into retirement. Seven-year-old African giant pouched rat, Magawa, has worked for most of his life detecting landmines in Cambodia. Light enough not to trigger the devices, he is able to scratch the top of the explosive to alert human handlers and is capable of searching a field the size of a tennis court in just 20 minutes. Over five years he sniffed out 71 mines in

total, along with dozens more dangerous, unexploded devices.

Trained in Tanzania by the charity Apopo to detect a chemical compound in the explosives, Magawa is one of the organisation's HeroRATs, with others from his cohort trained to detect tuberculosis.

Magawa became the first rat to be awarded the PDSA Gold Medal in the charity's 77-year history, for his 'life-saving devotion to duty'. This accolade is considered the animal equivalent of the George Cross – the highest award bestowed by the British government for non-operational gallantry. His retirement comes after his handler, Malen, said that his performance as a landmine detector has been unbeaten but that he had started 'slowing down' as he reached old age and that the time had come to 'respect his needs'.

Before retiring though, Magawa fulfilled one last act of duty – mentoring a batch of young rats who passed the Cambodian Mine Action Centre (CMAC) assessment and would be following in his pawprints. Speaking to the BBC about Magawa, Malen said: 'He is small, but he has helped save many lives, allowing us to return much-needed safe land back to our people.'

Glasgow to Plant a Tree
for Every Resident

Over the next decade, Glasgow is set to create an urban forest, planting a tree for every resident across the city region. Around 18 million trees will be planted in deprived areas, on the sites of former coalmines, on derelict land and in other civic areas. The Glasgow City Region, which consists of eight councils, already boasts around 29,000 hectares (112 square miles) of woodland, fragmented by urban development.

The project intends to connect these woodland spaces and boost biodiversity, allowing nature to thrive and increasing green cover from 17 to 20 per cent. Local authorities are rallying local businesses to participate in community tree planting projects and encouraging individuals and organisations to help identify places to plant new trees, or replace those that have been lost.

Speaking about the scheme, Councillor Andrew Polson, Chair of the Land Use and Sustainability Portfolio for Glasgow City Region, said: 'We all have a fantastic opportunity to work collectively to improve our living environment while tackling climate change at the same time.'

Supported by a £400,000 grant from the Woodland Trust's Emergency Tree Fund and £150,000 from

Scottish Forestry over the next two years, recruitment for a project team to start the new planting schemes is under way. The increased number of trees will absorb and store CO_2 emissions, improving the city region's air quality and contributing to the global fight against the climate crisis.

Mental Health Monitoring App Improves Patient Care

A new artificial intelligence (AI)-powered 'telehealth' app is changing the way that patients find support for mental health challenges. Telehealth is the delivery of healthcare, education and information services via remote technologies. The new app, created by Israeli start-up Mon4t, monitors four aspects of health – represented by the number four in the company's name – motor, cognitive, psychiatric and medical history.

Using state-of-the-art AI, the app acts as a toolkit to monitor motor aspects of mental health conditions, such as tremors or sense of balance; cognitive aspects, such as memory and reaction time and psychiatric aspects, such as how much time a patient stays indoors or spends outside. Patterns of behaviour are recorded alongside medical records, so that doctors have real-time information and a complete picture of their patient's condition and daily life, which cannot usually be accurately assessed in short clinical appointments.

This detailed knowledge allows for better care for patients and acts as an alternative to making clinical decisions based solely on doctors' subjective assessments. The app is already changing how patients and physicians interact with each other.

Mon4t also uses AI and smartphone technology to undertake brain monitoring and FDA-approved neurological tests for people with Parkinson's disease, paving the way for a telehealth revolution.

Plastic Book Sends Message to Future Generations

A creative agency in Vietnam has found an innovative way to use recycled plastic to send a message to future generations.

The team at Ki Saigon considered the fact that the plastic we throw away on a daily basis is still likely to be around when our great, great, great-grandchildren are born, on the basis that it takes hundreds of years to break down.

To highlight our current wastefulness and send a message of hope and optimism to future generations, the agency invited people all over the world to write letters to their imagined descendants, which would then be recorded in a book made from recycled plastic pages.

The pages were created by collecting different types of plastic bags, Styrofoam boxes, bubble wrap and plastic sheets, which were used for the base material. The plastics were then ironed between baking paper to fuse them together. Once set, each letter was scanned and hand-printed onto a page – preserving the handwriting of the original author – before the pages were hand-bound.

The project, Letters to the Future, generated an astonishing response, with the agency receiving 327 letters from 22 countries in just four months. The hand-crafted book is expected to last for more than 1,000 years, giving future generations ample time to take hope and comfort from the moving and inspiring messages within.

Hairy Heroes Save Lives at Sea

In the summer of 2021, eight children and their families were rescued from dangerous wind and wave conditions in Italian seas by some surprising hairy heroes – a trio of doggie lifeguards.

Working with their human trainers, three canine lifesavers called Eros, Mya and Mira were able to pull the potential casualties to shore in just 15 minutes, averting disaster. The three dogs were graduates of the Italian School of Water Rescue Dogs – La SICS Scuola Italiana Cani Salvataggio – or simply SICS – a team of 350 specially-trained canines who patrol 30 of Italy's busiest beaches, alongside their human colleagues.

Founder Ferruccio Pilenga came up with the idea for the school in 1989 when he was watching his dog – a sturdy Newfoundland called Mas – swimming powerfully in the sea. As well as being fearless, having significant stamina and being willing to perform, dogs also have finely tuned survival instincts, helping them to find the fastest and safest route back to shore.

Ferruccio decided to train dogs to become lifeguards and more than three decades later, an average of 20–30 people are rescued annually in Italy by his four-legged lifesavers, with the number increasing each year.

To become a doggie lifeguard, a pup has to undertake 18 months of basic training and only those who successfully complete the required steps are allowed to progress to the more advanced training that will allow them to become part of the elite SICS squadron. Advanced training includes intensive lifesaving techniques, jumping from helicopters and leaping from speeding boats into perilous seas.

These brave canines have been particularly lauded for their role in large-scale emergencies with multiple casualties as they are able to carry out the simultaneous rescue of multiple swimmers in situations where one or two lifeguards might find themselves overwhelmed. While Italy is currently the only country to recognise certified canine lifeguards, training centres are now being set up for dogs in the US, Germany, Switzerland and the Azores.

Fog-catching Nets to Hydrate the World's Driest Megacity

Fog-catching nets set up in the green hills surrounding the desert-based city of Lima, Peru, could supply its population of more than ten million people with water.

Lima is the world's driest megacity, experiencing less than an inch of rainfall every year. In recent years, global warming and climate change, combined with high levels of water consumption and low levels of rainfall, have posed a risk to water availability in the Peruvian capital, with water shortages becoming a concern. But one designer has sought to harness a unique feature of the city's weather to resolve this problem. Lima's location on the country's coast means that the surrounding hills are constantly covered by fog from the Pacific Ocean.

Alberto Fernandez came up with the idea of installing a 20 metre (60 foot) tower of spiralling nets to 'catch' the fog, after being inspired by simple two-dimensional fog nets installed by rural communities across South America.

While the rudimentary technology had flaws, Alberto found the basic principles to be sound and these have formed the basis for his own fog-catching nets. Alberto's nets are made of aluminium, wrapped in copper mesh and covered in plastic. Their towering structure, which can be built up to 200 metres (656 feet) high, allows them to collect water vapour from the clouds, while their spiral shape means that moisture-rich fog will always hit some part of the structure directly, regardless of wind direction.

The water collected will mainly be used for agriculture as it would need to be filtered for human consumption, but this will free up existing resources for use by Lima's residents. The innovation is cheaper than the desalination of seawater or filtering water from the River Rímac and – if enough towers and nets are installed – could collect as much as 1,000 litres (1,056 quarts) per day, and up to 3.6 million litres (3.8 million quarts) of water per year.

This invention is just one design to be featured in the Lima 2035 project, which aims to reverse trends of desertification (land dehydration in arid, semi-arid and dry sub-humid areas) and move towards climate resilience, agrobiodiversity and equitable access to resources.

Plastic Bottle Houses Prove to be Stronger than Brick

A state in north-western Nigeria has created a construction material that is thought to be 18 times stronger than regular bricks – using discarded plastic bottles.

A project in Kaduna is collecting empty plastic bottles and employing out-of-school or jobless young people to help construct the super-strong plastic bottle houses. The workers fill empty bottles collected from the streets with sand before they are stacked into a lattice pattern, bound together with mud using traditional techniques and finally secured with a net.

Referred to as bottle-brick technology, the houses comprise up to 14,000 bottles and their construction materials are more or less free. The method results not only in a striking-looking home, but also one that is strong and durable, and able to withstand even earthquakes.

Following its success in Kaduna, staff at the Development Association for Renewable Energies (DARE) are hoping to secure more funding for the project from the Nigerian government, so the scheme can be extended to employ more people, clean up more plastic waste and create more homes.

Landmark Ruling Allows Women to Co-own Ancestral Property

In India, ancestral property such as farms have traditionally been passed down along patriarchal lines, but one Himalayan state's decision could change this for good.

In March 2021, Uttarakhand became the first Indian state to give married women co-ownership of their husbands' ancestral property. The Uttarakhand Zamindari Abolition and Land Reforms Act will affect some 350,000 women who manage properties either alongside or in the absence of their husbands.

The latter has become more common as a result of a migration crisis, in which men in particular have been forced to leave their homes to seek work elsewhere, leaving their wives alone to run family farms. Agriculture has long been the foundation of Uttarakhand's economy and its local government made the ruling stating that it was unfair that despite carrying out most of the agricultural work, a woman was not able to make business decisions or apply for loans as the land was solely in her husband's name.

Chief Minister Trivendra Singh Rawa stated: 'We talk about equal partnerships and this ordinance will provide equal partnership to women. This will have a major impact and will go a long way in the overall development of the state.'

As well as providing married women with co-ownership of land, the Act also improves the right of divorced women. Provided they have no children with their first husband, divorced women will have a claim to co-ownership of their father's farm, and if a divorced husband becomes bankrupt, his ex-wife will also be able to file for co-ownership.

Local politicians have responded well to the landmark ruling and it is hoped that co-ownership rights will be extended to women in other Indian states in the near future.

Resources

Here are some fantastic resources for good news – keep reading and enjoying!

Good news titles:

Conscious Life News
Daily Encourager
DailyGood.org
Dezeen
Good News Network
Goodnet.org
Happiful
IFL Science
InspireMore.com
Optimist Daily
Positive News
Smiley News
The Happy Newspaper
Treehugger

Media with dedicated Good News sections:

BBC – Uplifting Stories
Huffington Post – Good News
LGBTQ Nation – Good News News
The Irish Journal – Good News
TheWeek.com – Good News
Today.com – Good News

Acknowledgements

With thanks to: University of Sussex, Optimist Daily, *The New York Times*, CNN, ApisProtect, HIVEOPOLIS, Fast Company, Signify, Wageningen University (WUR), *The Japan Times*, Japan Pom Pom, *Times of India*, Outside Online, Pink Bike, *Los Alamos Reporter*, Silver Stallion Bicycle & Coffee Works, Southwest Indian Foundation, Catena Foundation, Free Bikes 4 Kidz New Mexico, WUKA, Ruby Raut, CTGN Africa, Good News Network, North Sea Wind Power Hub programme, IFL Science, World Economic Forum, Danish Energy Agency, The Dublin Boys Club, *The Irish Times*, insauga.com, Zelpha Comics, UBB Babeş-Bolyai University, Romania Insider, AuREUS, James Dyson Awards, Dezeen, Love in a Bowl, South Africa The Good News, Dunedin City Council, Department of Conservation (New Zealand), Bridget Railton, Lexington Humane Society, UPI, WKYT, Rainbow Railroad, City Farmer, Cycloponics, Matador Network, Brighton and Sussex University Hospitals NHS Trust, BBC, Pink News, Kids 4 Change, ABC

News, *Riders West Magazine*, Bowhead Corp, EcoWatch, Purdue University Indiana, Chasing the Stigma, Jake Mills, Studio Roosegaarde, Conscious Life News, The Boston Medical Centre (BMC), Natural Products Global, Recover, Greenroofs.com, Luvely, Green Salon Collective, *Edinburgh News*, *Midlothian Advertiser*, *New Indian Express*, Manav Ekta Mission, Kidney Federation India, Accumulate, Do It Foundation, Grupo Do It, AM Costa Rica, *Tico Times*, The Gallatin, Anchor Rentals, Travel + Leisure, Spynes Mere nature reserve, Surrey Wildlife Trust, the *Guardian*, The Olive Press, Aponiente, the Nozomi Project, Huit Denim, Business-live.co.uk, Gizmodo, Visdeurbel.nl, University of California, Berkeley, StudyFinds, Reddit, Reuters, Project Milestone, The Construction Index, Crop Swap LA, Black Enterprise, Planetizen, Smiles 4 Miles, Pixie, Charlie Weatherstone (Luna), University Putra Malaysia (UPM), More Than Weeds campaign, Trillion Trees project, World Wide Fund for Nature (WWF), Birdlife International, the Wildlife Conservation Society (WCS), Duke University North Carolina, New Atlas, British Antarctic Survey (BAS), RNZ, Mini Mermaid Running Club UK, Free Conversations Movement, Readers Digest, The Connexion France, LEGO, The Independent, Office National de la Chasse et de la Faune Sauvage

(ONCFS), *National Geographic*, Phys.org, Eco Hub Cebu, Massachusetts Institute of Technology (MIT), CNN Philippines, Sproutworld, Cebu Daily News/Inquirer.net, Extra.ie, Assistive Technology Blog, AllWork, Caribos, Osaka University, The Arabic School of New Zealand, Daily Encourager, Oklahoma State University, We Are Mitú, Euro Group For Animals, Live Kindly, Treehugger, Via Ritzau, Animal Protection Index, South China Morning Post, Park Prescriptions (PaRx), Leeds Beckett University, The Wildlife Trusts, Big Think, Intelligent Living, Kyoto University Hospital, Prepwatch.org, World Health Organization (WHO), The Goldman Environmental Prize, The National Trust, Jeannette Heard, Wales 247, Natural Resources Wales, Algramo, *Stylist*, Halo Collective, *Personnel Today*, Tennessean, UN Environment Programme (UNEP), Stanford University California, *Sci Tech Daily*, Technology Networks, Safe In Austin, UniLad, CBS News, Good Morning America, *Victor Harbor Times*, Green Matters, Smartwool, Mental Floss, Fragments of Hope, Caribbean Culture + Lifestyle, LGBTQ Nation, *Gay Times*, *Rio Times Online*, InspireMore, The Falconer, VOA News, Qaz Japan, Sora News 24, Al Bawaba, Onomichi City Museum of Art, Little Island, Metro, Lonely Planet, LadBible, *Washington Post*, @thebionicbabe, CBC,

Australian Marine Parks, Euronews, Clean Yangon, Be One Percent, Pica Pica, Shine, Indian Express, Durham University, Earth.org, Greenpeace, Eco-business, Peequal, University of Göttingen, Dairy Global, Apopo, Glasgow Live, Goodnet.org, Ki Saigon, *Sculoa Italiana Cani Salvataggio*, Lima 2035.

And finally, thank you to my better half, Paul, who always reminds me to put down my phone, stop worrying and take time to appreciate the good in the world.